a daughter's promise

JoAnne Klimovich Harrop

Print ISBN: 979-8-35090-420-8
eBook ISBN: 979-8-35090-421-5

DEDICATION

This book is dedicated to my parents, my hero Paul Klimovich, my best friend Evelyn Klimovich, my brother, Paul Klimovich Jr., my uncle, Dario D'Antonio, and my very good friend, Darlene Lankiewicz.

Contents

Introduction 1

Chapter 1 – *The Call*..3

Chapter 2 – *Evelyn and Paul and Grandma, Too* 23

Chapter 3 – *The Lockdown Begins*.................................47

Chapter 4 – *The Shutdown* 67

Chapter 5 – *Perry*...84

Chapter 6 – *Bad News Just Keeps Coming*...................103

Chapter 7 – *About Me*...131

Chapter 8 – *The Long Goodbye* 146

Chapter 9 – *Alone* 164

Chapter 10 – *Life After Evelyn*..................................177

Chapter 11 – *Left Behind* 191

Chapter 12 – *Honesty*..209

The Final Thoughts 223

Acknowledgements 229

Introduction

THE WHEELCHAIR DIDN'T DEFINE MY mother.

In some ways, it emboldened her, making her more resolute than I'd ever seen her before.

Her journey to that wheelchair began Jan. 2, 2004 when a stroke took her ability to walk.

But it didn't take her spirit.

She'd fought bigger battles with an unshakable will and determination to survive.

And survive she did … when her dad walked out on her family when she was just a kid … when scarlet fever left her blind in one eye …when she lost the brother she loved so dearly in World War II and when she lost the baby she never had the chance to cradle in the nursery she'd prepared for him.

I sometimes wonder whether Evelyn Klimovich was the reason I became a sportswriter at a time when it was still a male-dominated business and women had to fight tooth and nail to get their fair share of assignments.

She never took the easy road and neither did I.

In the 1990s it was tough going out there for female sportswriters, but the joy of doing the job was so worth the sacrifice.

That's how Evelyn felt about her life, about raising five kids who all graduated from college and went on to successful lives.

It wasn't easy, but the happiness of seeing them thrive was so worth the sacrifices that she and my dad made to get us all there.

Evelyn was my hero, my best friend and my confidant.

She taught me about unconditional love, devotion and doing what is right, even when it hurts.

Growing up, we were far from rich, but Evelyn and my dad, Paul, gave me and my four siblings a blueprint for building caring relationships and being good, honest, hard-working people.

Paul and Evelyn were in this life together, through the good stuff and the bad, it was Paul and Evelyn against the world. Theirs was that once-in-a-lifetime love that we all dream of finding.

For 16-plus years after her stroke, I was her legs, pushing her everywhere in that wheelchair, logging more miles than I can count, criss-crossing Pittsburgh's neighborhoods, heading to church every Sunday without fail, eating at her favorite neighborhood hangouts and catching an occasional Pirates game at PNC Park on a summer afternoon.

Where I went, she wanted to go, and I wouldn't have had it any other way.

But in the spring of 2020, for Evelyn and me, the most daunting challenges were ahead.

JoAnne Klimovich Harrop

Chapter 1 –

The Call

ANOTHER FRIDAY WAS WINDING DOWN in the newsroom when my phone rang for what seemed to be the fiftieth time that day.

As I reached across my desk to answer, I stopped stone-cold for a split second when I saw the number of my mom's nursing home pop up on my screen.

In my heart, I knew why they were calling.

Off and on for about two months, we'd been publishing stories about this mysterious virus that took root in China, then spread to Japan and Thailand before landing in Washington State in January 2020.

Even as hundreds were dying in Asia, I think there was a sense of denial among some about it ever reaching us here in Pittsburgh. I don't know why, but there was.

For some, it seemed far away and out of mind.

Until it wasn't.

Until this day, when my phone rang just before 5 p.m.

It was March 13, 2020 ... Friday the 13th.

As I answered the call, there were a couple of things I knew for sure.

A week earlier, the first two cases of the virus now widely known as covid-19 were diagnosed in Pennsylvania – both hundreds of miles from Pittsburgh in Wayne and Delaware counties.

And on this day, as cases around the nation increased, Gov. Tom Wolf ordered our state's schools closed for 10 days beginning March 16.

Days earlier, rumors began circulating about the governor also shutting down the state's nursing homes to the public – possibly for as long as two weeks – to protect people like my 93-year-old mother, who'd been in a local facility for the past four years.

Though knee-jerk reactions to rumors usually aren't part of my makeup, I knew I needed a plan ... just in case.

There was too much at stake.

For the past 16 1/2 years, I'd cared for my mother after a stroke left her unable to walk and care for herself.

For the nearly five years since my dad died, I'd faithfully visited her every day after work, on vacation days and weekends.

It was a predictable and comfortable routine for both of us.

Most days, with her in her wheelchair and me parked in the closest straight chair, we'd start our time together with cookies or ice cream as she filled me in about her day, the latest nursing home gossip and chats with her best friend, Rosie Wyner, from three doors down the hall.

I'd tell her about the stories I'd written that day and the interesting people I'd met along the way.

Years earlier, I'd made the switch from sports to features, a move offering me an even better chance to use my writing and reporting skills to write stories about the patchwork of fascinating people and places in this diverse and vibrant city I call home.

Even when I'd had a tough day and just wanted to vent, my mom always listened intently, making me feel like I was the most important person on the face of the earth.

Some nights, we'd eat out, grabbing a bite at Big Jim's, her favorite hangout in our old Greenfield neighborhood, where everyone knew her name and her penchant for a hot bowl of Italian wedding soup.

JoAnne Klimovich Harrop photo
Evelyn enjoys her favorite soup at Big Jim's

Monday nights were our favorite at Big Jim's where a heaping plate of spaghetti was all ours for just 3 bucks.

Some days we'd talk sports.

Could this be the year the Pirates pull it all together and make it to the World Series for the first time since '79?

Who knew?

But Evelyn, as I'd started calling my mom at some point in my adult life, never lost her faith as a die-hard fan that it might just happen.

Most nights, like clockwork, we tuned in to "Jeopardy" at 7 p.m. followed by "Wheel of Fortune," impatiently shouting out answers as if the contestants could hear us.

And then there was the "Golden Girls."

Night after night, we watched the same reruns, laughing out loud at the predictable geriatric antics of Blanche, Dorothy, Rose and Sophia like we'd never seen the shows before.

In reality, I'd seen them so many times I could almost recite the dialogue by heart.

Without fail, Evelyn would start to doze off midway through the show, but still chuckle at the girls' missteps with her eyes half-closed.

The laughter was the best part. We always found a way to laugh, even during the toughest of times.

In my 50-some years of life, if I'd ever had a best friend, Evelyn Klimovich was it.

There was nothing I couldn't tell her, no problem too small or too big. When others in my life would send me packing, Evelyn always had time for me.

As the youngest of five kids and the only one living in Pittsburgh, I was the one who always was there for her.

And nothing, not even this dreaded virus was going to stop that.

So, on that day, when my phone rang, I knew what I had to do.

If the doors of her nursing home were closing for two weeks, I would stay with her – night and day – until those doors reopened.

Final decision.

No second thoughts.

Just Evelyn and me.

Twenty-four hours a day.

For two weeks.

Of course, that decision didn't just affect me.

My husband, Perry, the man whom I love for many reasons, may be among the few people in the world who understand my relationship with my family.

He understands because almost from the beginning, he formed the same relationship with them.

My family will suck you in and love you and you can't help but love them back.

Even when they defy all logic and make you crazy, you just have to love them because you know that when the chips are down, they're going to be there for you.

What more can you ask for in this life?

I can honestly say that there are days when we don't necessarily all like each other, but we love each other and we'll never turn our backs when one of us is hurting.

So with that said, Perry knew that if and when the doors of my mom's nursing home closed to the public, I'd be on the other side with her.

I already ran the logistics in my mind.

We had no children, so that wouldn't be a problem.

With the state's school buildings shutting down, including Perry's downtown Pittsburgh charter school, I knew he'd be busy with his own challenges, trying to teach his kids remotely when some of them didn't even have wi-fi.

I also knew he could cook and clean and take care of himself, so there were no worries about that.

I'd talked to my brother and three sisters, all living out of state, and they seemed grateful that I'd be with our mom as the virus spread.

Then it was time to talk with my editors.

Because I'd been with the newspaper for 20-plus years, I had enough PTO – paid time off – to handle this. Just in case I needed it, I filled out the paperwork for family leave.

My plan was in place.

So, on that Friday when the phone rang, I was ready.

All around me that day, reporters were on their phones, making calls to sources before deadline, typing and scribbling notes.

Each one seemed to be in his or her own world, oblivious to what was happening around them.

Editors were talking, yelling instructions across the room to photographers coming back from assignments and downloading photos into our system.

Police scanners were wailing in the background.

It's the type of organized chaos that occurs daily in most newsrooms and the type of atmosphere in which we all thrive.

The voice on the other end of my phone asked me, "How soon can you get here?"

It turned out that my mom's nursing home – Charles Morris Nursing and Rehabilitation Center in Pittsburgh's Squirrel Hill neighborhood – had decided to go into lockdown that day at 6 p.m.

The caller stressed that I needed to be there no later than 6.

Six days later, the governor would order all nursing homes in the state closed to visitors.

Suddenly, all of the noise around me was muted and for a minute, I was lost in the silence of my thoughts as I reviewed my mental checklist.

I knew it would take me at least 45 minutes to get to the nursing home.

It was 5 o'clock on a Friday … traffic might be heavy, but most of the traffic would be headed in the opposite direction out of the city, so I should be OK, I thought.

"I'm on my way," I said, slamming down the phone.

Suddenly, it all became very real.

I would be quarantining for two weeks with my mom in her nursing home, I thought to myself.

No problem.

I had to dash, because if I got there one minute late, I feared they wouldn't let me in.

My heart was racing.

To this day, I'm not sure what I said to my editor, Ben Schmitt, who was sitting near me.

I think I just shouted a casual, "I gotta go."

With people coming and going throughout the day in our newsroom, I don't think he realized it was the last time he'd see me for months.

Sheer adrenaline kept me moving, rushing past people in our building as I made my way through the Tribune-Review's lobby and to the parking lot where I jumped into the front seat of my SUV and headed out.

For some inexplicable reason, I thought it was a good idea to stop at a convenience store where I picked up a nonsensical array of goodies that included Arizona sweet tea, Twizzlers, Hostess cinnamon cakes, Frosted Flakes and sugar cookies.

I'm a picky eater and I guess I thought, worst case scenario, this assortment of sugary and incredibly unhealthy treats would sustain me for two weeks.

I wasn't headed into solitary confinement and Perry swore that he'd bring me anything I wanted, but it gave me comfort to have that junk food with me.

It was Lent or I would have grabbed lots of chocolate and 14 bottles of Mountain Dew – one for each of the days I'd be in quarantine.

Every year, I give up chocolate and Mountain Dew for Lent because I am a devout Catholic.

With Lent being a time of faith and reflection, we give up something that challenges us to live without. Every year, I manage to make it to Easter without breaking my Lenten promise.

I learned that from Evelyn. She believed in keeping promises.

But I was fairly sure that life without my chocolate and Mountain Dew would be doubly challenging during the next couple of weeks.

Somehow, I'd make it. I knew I would.

Knowing a lockdown might be looming, I'd been driving around for days with a stash of clothes and shoes in my back seat. I had more at the nursing home where I'd occasionally stay all night when my mother wasn't feeling well.

Anyone who knows me knows that I love fashion.

Hats and shoes are my true loves.

The bigger and more flamboyant the hats, the better. They're my signature accessory.

You seldom see me without some kind of hat perched on my head and flashy, dangerously high shoes on my feet.

But suddenly, none of that seemed so important.

I just needed to see my mother.

I was anxious about getting there, getting through the door and meeting my 6 p.m. deadline.

I wasn't worried about the lockdown. It was only for two weeks at the most, I thought as I navigated the Friday night traffic on the city streets, irritated every time I had to stop for a red light or another driver.

Overnight stays now and then with Evelyn had been no problem.

A few years ago, when she was fighting an infection, I'd slept on a padded windowsill in her room for several nights so I could be there if she needed me.

At the time, it didn't occur to me that this was odd. It just seemed like the best solution at the time.

After two weeks of antibiotics, she recovered.

I'd spent so many nights sleeping in contorted positions in chairs at my mother's side over the years, the windowsill didn't seem all that bad.

I admit that I was overprotective of her because she couldn't walk. She seemed so vulnerable.

For a woman as fiercely independent as my mother, not being able to get up and walk when and where she wanted was an enormous loss and it broke my heart.

I pictured her having to go to the bathroom in the middle of the night and no one coming to help. I imagined her trying to get there by herself and falling on the floor.

As I made my way to the nursing home, I stopped to fill up my car with gas. To this day, I'm not sure why I did because a road trip appeared unlikely any time in the next two weeks.

It's funny what we do in times of crisis.

I arrived at the nursing home at 5:59.

I have the printout to prove it.

One minute later and I might have been blocked from entering.

God really must have been my co-pilot that night.

I carried my purse, computer, bags of snacks, clothes, shoes and makeup into the building.

I heard the sliding doors close behind me.

It all seemed very surreal and a little frightening, mostly because of the unknown about what the next two weeks would hold for all of us inside this building.

Would the virus spread to Pittsburgh?

Would people inside this building get sick?

Would people die here?

Would I get sick?

How could I protect Evelyn?

There were signs on the doors that read: "STOP! Visitation for all non-staff & approved care providers is now restricted effective immediately."

One of the administrators was standing in the lobby.

"We've been waiting for you," he said.

He handed me a two-page document.

It was a waiver stating that if anything happened to me, the nursing home would not be responsible. I didn't even read it until later.

I just scribbled my name at the bottom of the last page.

I was in.

I noticed the halls were eerily quiet, especially for a Friday evening.

In the parking lot, I'd heard some residents' family members being told they weren't permitted to enter the building because of the lockdown.

I rode the elevator to the second floor … alone.

I rounded the bend and headed to see Evelyn in the Darlington wing – Room 208.

The floors and wings were named for notable people and places associated with the Pittsburgh area – Carnegie, Beechwood, Ellsworth and Allderdice.

The quiet walk to her room took me back to that first night – four years earlier – when I roamed the halls searching for my mom after she had been taken there by ambulance from UPMC Shadyside Hospital where she was treated for a broken hip.

On that night, the place seemed so overwhelming. I was lost and so was she. It was all so new and so foreign to both of us.

But in four years, my mom had found a home at Charles Morris. She felt safe there. And I felt safe having her there.

The staff was kind to her and to me.

I knew that while I was at work, they were watching over her.

Some became like family.

In the days ahead, I'd need that family.

And on that night, as I was about to walk away from everything in my life that I held precious – my home, my husband and my job – to spend the next two weeks locked down with my mother, I knew I needed to talk with her about what those days would be like for both of us.

As I entered my mother's room, I found her sitting in her wheelchair, snuggled under her favorite leopard print blanket, her back to me, watching the evening news on her small television.

She was wearing the blue sweater she loved so much. It matched her blue-framed glasses.

She was leaning on a tray table with her right arm holding up her head.

In front of her was a cup of thickened water, a box of Kleenex, the television remote and her cell phone.

Most of her liquids had to be thickened since her stroke to prevent her from choking.

The stroke, along with her advancing age, had taken a toll on her.

Always just a smidge over 5 feet tall, she seemed smaller every time I saw her these days.

Sometimes she repeated herself.

Often, she forgot things she never would have forgotten a year or two ago.

But still, she was sharp when it came to so many things.

That cell phone was everything to her and she was amazingly adept at using its intricate features. It was her link to the outside world and to me, so it always was at her side.

There were times she would call me several times a day to ask when I would be finished with work and when I thought I might be arriving there for my daily visit.

Often, she would say, "Can we go out for dinner?"

I usually replied, "yes."

But not on that first night of quarantine.

That night, the evening news was all about the virus and the mounting uneasiness around the world.

It was on that day when President Donald Trump declared a national state of emergency.

I kissed Evelyn on the forehead, gave her a hug and sat down on her bed to talk about what was happening.

We discussed what a quarantine meant.

We talked about the "virus."

I think she understood that we would be together for two weeks for some reason, but I'm not sure that she fully understood why.

This virus remained a bit of a mystery to her as it did to all of us.

Fourteen days didn't seem like such a big deal to us because we'd spent so many days together when Evelyn had her stroke and again when she broke her hip in a fall in 2016.

We comforted each other when my dad died in 2015.

We spent days crying because the three of us had done so much together.

Anytime one of my parents was in the hospital, I made sure they spent as much time together as possible because I saw the incredible sadness and palpable pain that overcame them when they were apart.

Jack Fordyce photo
JoAnne comforts her mother during her father's funeral.

They had been married for 66 years.

Evelyn's favorite photo of all time was their May 21, 1949, wedding picture, which was displayed on the ledge of that infamous windowsill where I once slept.

When dad died, she lost a piece of herself and so did I.

But we got through it and this time would be no different.

As long as we were together, that was all that mattered.

We settled in for the night with our matching Pittsburgh Steelers pillowcases and plenty of blankets because we were both always cold.

She had her single bed, and I had my cot that was delivered by a concerned nurse who said that if I ever decided to sleep on that windowsill again, she hated to think about what might happen if I took a tumble in the middle of the night.

We had that little TV to keep us company, though it had limited cable channels – Hallmark, Turner Classic Movies, TV Land – and anytime it stormed, the picture went black.

There was a channel that informed residents about activities and one where they could watch weekly Saturday Jewish services in the community room.

Charles Morris was operated by the Jewish Association on Aging, so the dining room menu featured traditional kosher foods, which, for the most part my mother enjoyed, especially the matzo ball soup, the kugel – a casserole commonly made with noodles – and the babka – a sweet, braided bread with cinnamon.

But the staff was ever-mindful of my mother and me – two devout Catholics – and always tried to provide us with other foods we might enjoy.

Our room wasn't fancy, but it was enough.

A blue recliner sat in the corner, two brown dressers held clothes for both of us, a single lamp helped illuminate the room along with an overhead light.

The windowsill was loaded with family photos with storage underneath that was packed with the snacks Evelyn enjoyed so much.

We each had an adjustable tray table with wheels for our meals.

There was a bathroom, but no shower.

The shower down the hall was for the residents, and now it was for me, as well. I had to wait my turn until after all the residents had their showers before I could use it.

Growing up the youngest of five kids in a seven-person household with one bathroom, I was used to waiting.

That first night, I got my mom ready for bed and then looked around.

We would be OK.

I knew we would.

My mind was whirling with all kinds of thoughts.

Thoughts of the day.

Thoughts of the virus.

Thoughts of the unknown.

Thoughts of my dad.

He was never far from my mind, but on that night, he was with me more than usual.

The day we buried my dad, I cried harder than I thought any human possibly could.

The tears came and wouldn't stop, and I made no apologies to anyone for them.

It was my dad and the thought of never seeing him again, of never hearing his voice or just knowing he was there for me was almost more than I could imagine.

I know that as a woman in her fifties, I should have been ready for this, right?

We should all be ready to lose our parents one day. It's just the cycle of life.

But how do we do that?

It's not that simple.

How do we prepare ourselves to lose the people who not only brought us into this world and nurtured us along the way, but also loved us unconditionally, regardless of the screwups we made along the way?

As age began to rob my mom and dad of the simplest of everyday functions and joys, I was with them every step of the way – pushing them in their wheelchairs when their legs would no longer support them and acting as their advocate when their minds could no longer navigate the ins and outs of the medical world.

I loved spending time with them. I laughed at their stubbornness and how they seemed to fight the notion of getting old.

I loved seeing their endless devotion to each other play out in front of me. I marveled at their bond and how at times, they almost seemed to function as one person.

A lifelong friend and former teacher, Cindy McNulty, said everyone in Greenfield considered them such a team that their names – Paul and Evelyn – seemed to blend together as one word.

They were simple people who found joy in the simplest things that life had to offer.

My mom had an amazing attitude about life, despite everything she'd been through.

She loved often and she loved hard.

Her husband, five kids, seven grandchildren and two great-grandchildren were everything to her.

After she was gone, four more great-grandchildren arrived who unfortunately will only get to know their amazing great grandma through the stories they will hear from the rest of us who loved her so much.

When those kids or grandkids found love, it was the greatest source of happiness for her.

She never drank and never smoked.

Her not-so-secret indulgences were strawberry ice cream, anything cinnamon, chocolate chip cookies, and hot coffee first thing every morning.

She wore turtlenecks on 90-degree days, pants with elastic waistbands and warm socks.

For her, it was always function over fashion.

Makeup and Chanel No. 5 were for special occasions – Mass and family gatherings.

She worked hard raising her kids and when I was about 8, she went back to work outside the home, which devastated me, but with five kids we needed the money.

She took on a number of odd jobs, even working at the iconic Pittsburgh fast-food restaurant, Winky's, where she arrived before dawn each day to make the doughnuts at one of the chain's downtown Pittsburgh locations.

My dad spent his life working hard, most of it in tire shops around the city. He always seemed to have a job or two on the side to keep things going at the house.

We didn't have a lot, but we never felt poor.

His only guilty pleasure was golf, which he was able to play for not too much money at the old Schenley Park public course, a few minutes from our house.

His prized possession was a bright green jacket, the same color as the one given to the winner of the Master's golf tournament – even made by the same company. It was a gift to him from his kids one year on Father's Day. We couldn't imagine anything else that would make him happier.

And so it was that all those memories and more came flooding back as I stood there in the parlor of the Edward P. Kanai Funeral Home in my best black dress and oversized black hat with polka dot detail, trying to get through it all, trying to say goodbye to my dad for the very last time.

It is a big white sprawling funeral home with stately white pillars and a black turret on a well-manicured corner lot where so many in Pittsburgh's Greenfield neighborhood have sent their loved ones to be buried for generations.

Like my dad, a lot of folks in Greenfield don't have much money, but they work hard all their lives and when they hand their loved ones over to Kanai's, they know their funerals will be handled with grace, dignity and a personal touch by the fourth generation of Kanai family members running the business.

But all of that was lost on me at that moment.

All that I could do was cry.

It was that time that every daughter dreads, that moment when her dad, the first man she ever loved, passes on to the next life, a life that hopefully is free of the pain my dad endured during the last several years while undergoing dialysis three times a week as he tried so desperately to hang on.

He didn't want to leave my mother, and he told doctors he'd do anything to avoid it.

He was a fighter.

As a young man, he stormed the beaches at Normandy on D-Day and as thousands around him died, he managed to survive through sheer grit and determination.

He was sure he could do it again because he couldn't bear the thought of Evelyn being alone.

He had setbacks in life, but he always made it through, usually with Evelyn at his side. It was the two of them against the world.

Almost 70 years earlier, he fell in love with her across the floor of a crowded dance hall and he wasn't ready to say goodbye, and neither was I.

But God had other plans and on June 6, 2015, 71 years to the day after he came ashore at Normandy, he took his last breath.

He was so proud of his country and his service to it, though he seldom talked about the atrocities of war.

In his casket, he wore a U.S. flag tie, the hat from his days in the service at his side.

Four U.S. Army emblems were affixed to his casket. He was buried with full military honors.

And on that Saturday, on the day of his funeral, I will never forget that moment when it was time for our family to let him go.

One by one, my siblings and I filed forward to his casket to say goodbye.

First, Rose, then, Paula, then Ruth, then me. My brother Dave pushed our mother in her wheelchair. She looked so heartbroken and so tiny as she gazed down at my dad with a look of deep sadness in her eyes I had never seen before.

It was just us – my brother, sisters, me, our spouses and my mom, alone in the room with my dad – the way it had been so many times before.

I couldn't speak.

I didn't have to.

Earlier, I said my final words to my dad in a note I wrote to him, my hand shaking with every stroke of the pen.

I'm a writer. It's all that I truly know to do in times of crisis.

When spoken words have eluded me, written words have never failed me.

When I am happy, my joy is best expressed through my writing. When I am sad, my sadness often is softened by putting pen to paper. When my heart is broken in a thousand pieces as it was when my dad died, the process of healing begins with writing my sometimes ragged, rambling thoughts.

I looked at him in that casket and knew that inside the pocket of that bright green Master's blazer that he loved so much was the note I had slipped to the funeral director that morning.

It was there, in that jacket, right next to his favorite putter that we planned to bury with him, just in case he needed it.

Through my tears, I had carefully folded the note in half and asked the funeral director to tuck it into my dad's breast pocket, next to his heart.

I never told anyone about it. I just couldn't talk about it.

It was just between my dad and me and had remained that way until now.

It was this daughter's promise to her dad that even after he was gone, she would do all that she could do to make sure that the love of his life was safe and sound until they could be together again.

"Dad, I will always love you," the note read. "You will forever be my hero. You loved Evelyn with all your heart. I promise that I will take care of her. "

Now, it was up to me to keep the most important promise of my life.

Chapter 2 –

Evelyn and Paul and Grandma, Too

THAT FIRST NIGHT IN QUARANTINE, against a backdrop of muffled hallway voices and creaking medicine carts passing by, I lay on the folding cot next to my mother's bed, staring at her as she slept, watching her every breath, thinking about the days ahead for her, but also about the days behind her.

Life had thrown so much at Evelyn, but she always put one foot in front of the other and kept moving with that unbreakable spirit I knew would help us through the next 14 days.

I'd always hoped she'd passed on some of that strength to me.

But there were times when I wasn't sure if I was nearly as strong as this woman who had borne so much hardship but put those days aside to relish all the good that life had delivered to her – the gentle, kind-hearted man who loved her with every shred of his being and the five kids who adored her.

But it seemed that God always was testing her.

Almost from the moment she was born, she faced the cold ... the cruel ... the unthinkable ... and at times, the kind of heartbreaking grief that would destroy many of us.

But not Evelyn.

I'm not sure she realized it, but this pandemic-in-the-making that we were facing was just the latest test thrown her way and mine.

I'd protect her.

I had to.

I promised I would.

In 1935, when Evelyn was just 8, a case of scarlet fever wracked her tiny body, sickening her for months and leaving her blind in one eye.

From time to time, as an adult, she'd talk about being locked in a room at her mother's house for months out of fear that she'd infect her brothers and sister.

When she finally was able to leave the room, her heart was broken when a ragged little doll that was her only companion during her illness was taken from her and destroyed because of concerns it might carry the disease.

But even then, she felt lucky – lucky to be alive, she recalled.

Scarlet fever, with its red, sandpaper-like rash still was killing children in the 1930s, but not as many as it did at the turn of the century when it reached epidemic proportions.

By the time Evelyn contracted the disease, the advent of antibiotics had reduced its deadly effects.

Although it was a long road to recovery, she fought hard, regaining her strength and adjusting to the loss of vision in her left eye, which she seldom ever mentioned throughout the remainder of her life.

Even as a child, when life seemed to take more than it gave, Evelyn never wavered from her belief that it was all part of God's master plan.

But not long after her bout with scarlet fever, life kicked her again when her father, Alfredo D'Antonio, walked out the door one day and never returned, leaving her mother and her three siblings to fend for themselves.

It was a cruel turn of events that would prove life-changing for all of them.

My mother's devastation had nothing to do with the sudden, unexplained loss of her father from her life.

She'd always been clear that she didn't particularly like him, let alone love him.

He'd been cold and distant, showing no affection to the four children he brought into this world.

Her deep sadness stemmed from what his abrupt departure did to her mother, whom she dearly loved.

I can't say for sure, but I've always had my suspicions that theirs was an arranged marriage, not one built on love, but maybe on the hopes that it would grow into love.

After he left, my mom and the other kids occasionally would visit him on Sundays, but he showed little interest in them, making them sit perfectly still for hours, never speaking with them while he entertained other guests.

His children truly meant nothing to him, my mother would say with a rare bitterness in her voice.

Eventually, he moved to Michigan, where we believe he started another family.

All contact with his Pittsburgh family ceased and Evelyn would never see him again.

Like my mother, my grandmother, Maddalena D'Antonio, was a strong woman who came to the United States from Naples, Italy on Nov. 23, 1923, carrying not much more than the clothes on her back and her first-born, 1-year-old Danny. Her long and arduous journey took her to Boston first, then to Pittsburgh.

In those days, immigrants eager to fit in when they arrived in the U.S., often Americanized their names and the names of their children. Little Danny's birth name was actually Dario.

Upon her arrival, she spoke only a few words of English but worked hard to learn the language of her new country.

They joined my grandfather who came to the U.S. before them, settling in Bellevue, a working-class community north of Pittsburgh, where he'd found a job as a laborer for the borough.

Bellevue meant "beautiful view" in French and by all accounts it truly was a beautiful sight for my grandmother and the other immigrants who'd settled there, patronizing the dozens of small specialty shops lining the town's bustling main street.

While my grandmother stayed home, filling their home with the rich aroma of hearty Italian foods and tending to Danny, my grandfather went off to work.

A second son, John, was born in 1925, then Evelyn in 1927, followed by Lucy in 1929.

Klimovich Family photo
From left, Evelyn poses with her brothers, Dario and John and sister, Lucy, along with their mother, Maddalena D'Antonio.

After my grandfather left, my grandmother did everything humanly possible to make sure her children had all they needed.

Her life became a seemingly endless, exhausting cycle of work, seldom taking time to rest or do for herself.

She cleaned houses. She took in boarders. Though my mother and her brothers and sister were young, they helped in any way they could.

"My mother didn't have an easy life," my mom said to me on more than one occasion. "She did what she had to do to take care of us. She scrubbed floors. We had hand-me-downs. She was tough."

The kids grew up quickly.

My Aunt Pat, my Uncle John's wife, remembers that as a young married woman, my mom was very serious.

"Maybe she felt like she had to be more grown-up because there was no dad there," Aunt Pat said.

Though just keeping food on the table and a roof over their heads was a challenge, my grandmother remained steadfastly committed to making sure her kids received an education.

She scraped together the money for all of the kids to attend Assumption Elementary School, a Catholic school in Bellevue, but there was no money for my mom to attend Catholic high school, which was crushing because she desperately wanted to learn.

A pastor stepped in and paid for her to attend Mt. Assisi Academy in Bellevue, an all-girl's school.

It was an exciting time for her.

She loved school and quickly made friends with the girls there.

A photo I treasure shows her being named to the school's May Court.

But it also was a tumultuous time in the world around her.

As my mother's high school years were about to begin, the Japanese bombed Pearl Harbor and the U.S. entered World War II.

Eventually, the boys my mom grew up with, including her two brothers, went off to serve.

All that my grandmother, my mom and her sister could do was wait and worry.

With Danny and John off to war, suddenly my mother was the oldest child at home and was forced to be the strong one, not only for my grandmother, but also for her younger sister.

News from the battles raging around the world trickled in.

Families huddled around radios hoping to hear something … anything about bloody conflicts that took their loved ones so far away from them.

Letters arrived, but they were few and far between.

One day, as the Battle of the Bulge raged between December 1944 and January 1945, soldiers appeared on my grandmother's doorstep to tell her that Danny, the little boy she'd carried with her from Italy on a ship called the *Arabic* was "missing in action."

They came back the next week.

Danny was dead.

He was 22.

My grandmother fell to her knees, my mother said.

She wanted a proper burial for him, she told these uniformed men who delivered the most crushing news of her life.

But she would be denied that final goodbye.

The soldiers told my grandmother that Danny's body could not be returned to her until after the war.

Heartbroken and angry, she told them to let him rest in peace where he died.

To my knowledge, neither my mother nor my grandmother knew the location of that final resting place, information lost in the chaos of war and my grandmother's grief.

In the end, all that she'd ever have to show for her beautiful boy was one of his dog tags and a few personal belongings the Army sent along after his death.

As I worked with my now retired executive editor, Sue McFarland, on this book, the loose ends surrounding my uncle's death bothered both of us.

Maybe it was because we are journalists. Maybe it was because it was a piece of my family history that had remained a mystery for so long.

Sue searched government records to see what she could find about Danny.

We wanted to know more, but there was so little to discover because his life was so brief.

One Saturday morning in November, Sue sent me a note telling me she'd found something about him on a government registry containing the following brief entry, information I know my mother never had:

Private Dario D. D'Antonio
Date of Death: November 30, 1944
413th Infantry Regiment, 104th Infantry Division
Buried – Plot A Row 15
Henri Chapelle American Cemetery
159, rue du
Memorial American
4852
Hombourg, Belgium
Awarded: Purple Heart

Through additional research, Sue was able to provide even more information that gave me historical perspective about my uncle's death, the pivotal battle that claimed his life and the cemetery where his remains are buried. Later, she sent a photo of the headstone on his grave.

I felt a sense of relief that 79 years after Danny died on that battlefield, the niece he never met could honor his memory by writing about him in her book.

Though he'd never had a funeral, never had a hero's welcome home and never had a chance to live his life, I could write that Danny died a hero in Belgium in the days leading up to the bloody battle that would mark the beginning of the end for the Germans in World War II.

And he was buried along with 8,000 other American soldiers and allies not far from where he fell on a battlefield in eastern Belgium.

However, in reality, none of that would have mattered to my grandmother.

All that ever mattered was that her Danny was gone.

And for my mother, all that mattered was that the kid who never wanted to go to war, the gentle, peaceful one whose greatest joy came from helping his younger brother and sisters with their homework, was never coming home.

My grandmother was never the same, never got over his death, never stopped grieving until the day she died, my mother said.

I think that on some level, my mother never got over losing Danny either.

About a dozen years after Danny died, my grandmother moved to Florida, where she lived out her life until old age and sickness took her from us in 1986 when she was 82.

She'd met a man named Sam Butch while she was cleaning houses back in Pittsburgh.

He moved to Florida, bought a beautiful home and lived his dream of owning orange and grapefruit groves there. She followed him and they lived together, running what became a successful business.

My older relatives insist there was nothing romantic, that they were just good friends, but I do know those were some of the best days of my grandmother's life.

I'm glad she found Sam, who always was so happy to see us when we visited.

Though it took a lifetime, my grandma found her joy with Sam.

She deserved that joy and more.

And when she died, I suppose she finally was at peace, knowing she would be reunited with her Danny once again.

The two of them would be together, as they had been when they came from Italy so long ago.

My mother didn't wait as long as my grandmother to find her joy in life.

With high school graduation looming, she had a plan.

Of course, she had no idea how to execute that plan, but she knew she'd find a way.

For a woman graduating from high school in the 1940s with no money, her options were somewhat limited, but that didn't stop her.

She set her sights on business school where in a relatively short time she could learn the skills she needed to find a job in one of those big downtown Pittsburgh office buildings that she passed so often but never entered.

She was accepted to what was then the Robert Morris School at the old William Penn Hotel in downtown Pittsburgh where she learned shorthand and other office skills. It was enough to land her that first job at an insurance company doing filing, typing and taking shorthand.

It was an exciting life for her, earning her own money, riding the streetcar into the city each day and of course, helping her mother, who continued to struggle back at their house along Ohio River Boulevard in Bellevue.

Even though the nation's economy was limping through its post-war recovery, life was looking up for Evelyn.

On weekends, she and her friends would go to a dance hall in nearby West View. It was a time when the music of Peggy Lee, Bing Crosby, Vaughn Monroe and Vic Damone topped the charts.

One night in 1948, she saw a good-looking guy – not too tall, but tall enough – across the room.

I should mention that my mom was never a shrinking wallflower.

At just barely 5 foot 2 inches tall back then, she'd always had a way of making her presence known.

If she was thinking something, she said it. If she wanted something, she went after it.

So, on that night, she strolled up to the young man, whose name she learned was Paul Klimovich, and asked him to dance, something that young ladies just didn't do much back then.

Nonetheless, he obliged.

She was 21.

He was 26.

He'd also lost his father, but under much different circumstances in a work-related accident.

The scars of 11 months of bloody combat in Europe were still very fresh for my dad, whose mind replayed the horrors of the battles he fought over and over again like a movie with no ending.

He survived because he could dig a foxhole faster than anyone else, he told my mother.

He recalled the harrowing tale of making his way through enemy territory after his fellow soldiers left him for dead in a foxhole where he lay motionless, hoping to fool attacking Germans. But he came back alive as did his four brothers.

That first night they talked, danced and laughed.

The conversation was easy, almost like they'd known each other for years.

She liked him, but he said he didn't really like to dance, which gave her reason to pause.

He was smitten with her, so he returned to that dance hall week after week to search her out and ask her to dance again and again.

They would remain dancing partners for 66 years.

A year after that first meeting, they were married – my mom in an ornate lace wedding gown, a cascading veil that encircled her dark hair and matching gloves that stretched to her elbows and my dad in a striking dark tuxedo – in a ceremony at Assumption Roman Catholic Church in Bellevue on May 21, 1949.

They honeymooned at Niagara Falls and rented an apartment on

Pittsburgh's North Side, then shortly afterward bought a newly built, three-bedroom house on Stanley Street in the city's Greenfield section where they'd start the family of their dreams.

Their lives were falling into place.

Like Bellevue, Greenfield, on the east side of the city, was a middle-class neighborhood with a mix of Italians and Irish, although my dad, who was Polish, was an outlier. It didn't matter, everyone was welcome in Greenfield.

The irony of their new address on Stanley Street was not lost on my dad, whose older brother Stanley had been killed when he was hit by a car while riding a homemade skateboard when they were kids.

Soon after moving into their new house in 1950, my mother discovered she was pregnant with their first child.

It was a joyous time for them as they planned for the baby's arrival.

If it was a boy, he would be named Paul Jr.

My dad was so proud.

There would be a son to carry on his name.

But tragedy would strike again.

Paul Jr. was born with a heart defect.

He lived one month.

They held a service for him at the Kanai Funeral Home in Greenfield, the same place that would handle my parents' funerals and probably will handle mine, if it's still around.

They buried Paul Jr. in Calvary Cemetery in Hazelwood where they also bought plots for themselves.

After that, Evelyn assumed they would never have children.

It was not God's plan.

She was wrong.

Really wrong.

My oldest sister Rose arrived in 1953, followed by Dave in 1956.

On June 5, 1959, my parents got two surprises of a lifetime.

A very pregnant Evelyn yelled for my dad to come into the bathroom.

There, he delivered my sister Paula, whom they named after him.

My mother called Dr. George Olah, who came to the house to look after the baby and my mother.

When he arrived, she told him she wasn't feeling well.

He said, "There might be another baby in there."

"Get me to the hospital," she told the doctor.

He was right.

There were twins.

Our oldest sister, Rose, who was about 6 at the time, recalled the scene as chaotic.

My dad cradled Paula and introduced her to Rose and Dave then took the two of them to a neighbor's house.

The police drove my mom and Paula to Mercy Hospital where she delivered Paula's twin, Ruth.

My mom always said, "God gave me two babies after losing my first one."

Ruth came home from the hospital after a week.

Paula stayed longer because she was so small. She was baptized in the hospital as a precaution.

The story made the Pittsburgh newspapers' front pages and the evening television news broadcasts.

Four years later, on July 17, 1963, I was born.

They always said I was planned, but I'm not sure.

My dad was 42 and my mom was 36.

Having five kids at any age is a lot, but by the time I came along, they were considered to be much older than many other parents of newborns.

When I was older, sometimes people would mistake them for my grandparents.

But for me, their ages were irrelevant. They were tireless and loving parents.

With my arrival, Paul and Evelyn finally had the big family they dreamed of when they first married.

It was in that family that Evelyn finally found her joy.

And that family, as loud and crazy as it could be, always was their priority.

With all of those kids to keep track of, Evelyn and Paul not only had to be parents, but they also had to be cops.

They slept in a first-floor room, so they always knew when we came in the door.

There were rules, some of them arbitrary, some of them silly, but with that number of kids, someone had to be in charge.

We couldn't get a driver's license until we were 17. Even though the state said 16 was OK, Evelyn didn't like it. It was 17 in her mind. Take it or leave it, she told us when we whined about it.

When the time came to learn to drive, our dad taught us. No driver's ed for us. We learned at Schenley Park at the golf course. He was patient beyond words.

We had to be home when the streetlights came on with no questions asked. When we complained, Evelyn told us, "Someone has to be first."

End of discussion, she'd say.

When we were allowed to get a treat from the ice cream truck on Tuesdays because it was payday, she'd get mad when we wanted to buy red, white and blue Popsicles because, "we have Popsicles in the freezer."

But there were rules and traditions that I remember and cherish to this day.

Dinner was eaten together as a family. No excuses.

When we were really lucky, those dinners featured Evelyn's homemade meat ravioli, a recipe passed down from her mother.

There were always presents under a live tree on Christmas morning – no artificial trees for the Klimovich family.

And there were new clothes for all of us for the first day of school, although I have no idea how my parents paid for it all.

And I can still taste my mom's homemade doughnuts. We each played our role in that project as we placed the hot doughnuts in brown bags filled with powdered sugar and cinnamon and shook them until they were covered with a fine dust of sweetness.

It was nirvana in a bag.

Without fail, Paul and Evelyn approached everything that life threw at them together.

Every decision, from the most insignificant to the most important, was made as a team.

They always knew how to solve a problem – together.

In the spring of 1967, our dad was working a side job and fell off a roof, breaking his leg and dislocating his elbow.

With no money coming in, they had to come up with a plan to keep things together at the house.

My mother went to the utility and mortgage companies to tell them they couldn't pay their full bills for a few months until he got back to work. She promised that it was a short-term setback. It seemed to work.

Life went on. The lights stayed on and there was food on the table every day.

When he was released from the hospital, she took care of him, nursing him back to health and keeping everything around the house running like clockwork until he could return to work.

My siblings all remember that incredible sense of teamwork that seemed to be their weapon against any hard times.

"There were no secrets," my sister, Paula Montanez, said from her home outside of Nashville where she lives with her husband, Josue, a radiologist she met while working as a nurse in Cleveland.

"It is hard to compare it to something, but if you look at what they did and how we all turned out, I think they were very good parents," said my oldest sister, Rose Klimovich, who did her undergraduate work for two years at Penn State and graduated with both an undergraduate degree in math and economics and an MBA from Carnegie Mellon University before going on to a number of corporate leadership jobs in product management, marketing and strategy in New Jersey and New York, where she now lives.

Education was a priority as we grew up.

My brother Dave studied chemical engineering at Case Western Reserve University and earned a master's degree in materials science and engineering from the University of Pittsburgh.

Paula studied nursing at Case Western Reserve University.

My sister Ruth Rooney studied theater at Point Park University, and I have a degree in marketing from Penn State.

Klimovich Family photo
The Klimovich family visits Hershey in 2001. From left, JoAnne, Paula, Paul, Evelyn, Rose, Dave and Ruth (in front).

In the summers, we were always doing something to learn.

Evelyn would put us in separate rooms to read and write or do something productive.

Our dad would drop us off at Carnegie Library and Carnegie Museum in Oakland and come back five hours later to pick us up.

We only learned in later years that he went golfing while we were there.

Although they didn't know a lot about college life, they did everything they could to get us in the door and keep us there.

They didn't have the money to help with tuition or room and board, but they helped us with the applications and paperwork to get loans and grants.

They sat with us as we signed up for work-study jobs.

With five kids, every penny was important.

"They truly were a team," said my sister Ruth, who with her husband, Gregg, pursued acting careers for a while in New York before moving to New Jersey. "They divided and conquered. They had different strengths."

"I remember the family picnics and mom taking two buses and then having to walk to get to my swim meets," said Ruth, who now runs a health club in New York. "Those are the things you remember."

Ruth said she always tells her daughter, Violet, that "you will not remember what we gave you, but you will remember the things we did for you."

My brother Dave, who lives in Mentor, Ohio, with his wife Cindi, said our summer trips to Dade City, Fla. near Tampa, to visit Evelyn's mother are still among his favorite family memories.

Mom would pack the car and get us ready, and dad would go to the AAA to get a TripTik map, so we knew the route. We would stop in Charlotte, N. C. overnight where my godmother, Donna Cline, lives.

We had our assigned seats in the car.

Dave and Rose would sit on the back seat.

Paula and Ruth were on the floor in the back.

I would fit nicely in the back window.

I was only about 5 or 6 at the time and I have to admit that I made out on that deal because I had a lot more space on that back window than the six others had crammed in that Ford Galaxy 500 that my dad drove on many of those trips.

It did get hot back there with the sun beating down on me, but the fun and the anticipation of getting to our destination far outweighed any discomfort I experienced.

Through it all, we learned so much about living from those trips and from our parents.

"Mom and dad were committed to each other, and to the marriage and to the family," Dave said. "It is kind of a neat thing, and you don't see it as much now. People just give up on each other."

Not our parents. No way.

On those trips down south, we started the ride with prayer, a Hail Mary and an Our Father for safe travels. We didn't have suitcases. Our clothes were packed in boxes. We ate cereal out of packages and lots of peanut butter and jelly sandwiches. We played the "license plate game" and "count the Volkswagen Beetles" along the way to entertain ourselves. It kept us busy for hours.

When we arrived, our dad would take us to Lake Iola to swim. That gave my mom some alone time with her mom.

Our grandmother, a slightly built woman with a thick Italian accent, would greet us at the car, waving her hands in the air and yelling, "you're late! Where ya been?"

It didn't matter how early you might be, she'd always insist that you were late, but always follow up with, "you wanna a nice pasta. I make-a it for you!"

She was quite a character, but oh, how we loved that woman and our trips to visit her.

Klimovich Family photo
**The Klimovich kids pose with Evelyn on a Florida vacation in the 1970s at their grand-
mother's home.**

We'd eat her homemade pasta and pick oranges and grapefruit from the trees
she had on the land she and Sam tended.

For kids born and raised in the North, those fresh fruits tasted like
candy to us. I can still taste those oranges and feel the juice running down
my chin as I devoured them.

But those trips weren't without their missteps.

We went to Walt Disney World in Orlando just after it opened in the
1970s, never imagining it might have reached its capacity on any given day.

You can only imagine our excitement.

We pulled into the parking lot and were told it was full.

We all cried.

Paul and Evelyn took us to breakfast and went back to the park later to give it another try.

We got in and the day was saved.

It's funny how I still remember the details of those trips like it all happened yesterday.

Each time, as we packed the car to leave for home, our grandma would load any empty space with fruit. A quick stop or a sharp turn would send oranges flying everywhere.

And once, on our way home when I was a little girl, we stopped at a restaurant for lunch. I left my baby doll, Karen, in the booth.

I never knew back then that the name Karen would get such a bad rap today or I might have rethought that approach.

We'd been on the road at least 20 miles when I remembered.

My dad turned around, and when he went into the restaurant, there was Karen, slouched down in the booth.

To this day, my siblings hold this against me.

I am not sure where that doll is today, but I'm sure that not many dads would have done what mine did.

In all my life, I only saw my mother cry four times – when her brother John died, when her mother died, when my dad died and when she had her stroke in 2004.

My uncle, my grandmother and my dad were the three constants in her life, the people who were there for her through it all.

And on some level, despite her indomitable spirit, she knew that her stroke signaled a loss – the loss of her fiercely guarded independence.

But despite the tears, she refused to let it stop her.

She worked hard to get stronger with physical and occupational therapy and continued to improve her speech with a speech therapist.

Being confined to a wheelchair changed her life – and our family members' lives – dramatically.

I was working a 4 p.m. to 11:30 p.m. shift at the Tribune-Review as a sportswriter. I would spend pretty much every day with my parents, who still were living in their Greenfield home.

I made sure they had their meals and did some cleaning. There were times I would return after work and stay overnight if they had early medical appointments.

A few days a week my mom went to outpatient therapy, so I rode with her on a specially equipped, accessible bus to get there.

That gave my dad an opportunity to golf and relax a bit. Despite my help, the stress of my mom's stroke was beginning to show, and we all worried about his health.

Taking care of her and the house and all that came with it was beginning to be too much.

In 2008, my sister Paula told them that they needed to move from their house to an assisted-living facility. She did the leg work and found Schenley Gardens in the city's Oakland section, not far from the University of Pittsburgh campus.

They didn't fight us. I think in their minds, they knew it was time to move and they were doing it together, so that helped.

We celebrated one final Christmas in our house. It was a time when the memories rushed back – of going to bed on Christmas Eve dreaming of what gifts we'd receive on Christmas morning.

Despite not having much money, they always made sure there were piles of wrapped presents and an abundance of joy in that modest living room of ours.

When I told their next-door neighbors, Nancy and Ed Regan, that my parents were leaving, Nancy said she couldn't watch us drive away.

We hadn't planned well for the move.

Not much was packed by moving day.

Maybe subconsciously I thought that if I didn't pack, I wouldn't have to leave the house where we had so many great memories?

The movers did an amazing job of saving the day by getting pretty much everything we wanted packed and moved to Schenley Gardens.

My mom and dad had a large, one-bedroom corner apartment and they were so happy to have tons of people around them all the time and a slate of activities to enjoy.

They formed an immediate bond with one aide, Christine Ellis, who called them Miss Evelyn and Pops.

In her spare time, Christine went everywhere with us on our family outings – to church, to the casino, to Big Jim's, even to the Pirate games.

"I loved your family. I loved your parents. Pops and Miss Evelyn were role models. They gave me a lot of encouragement and I felt like I was part of the family," she told me later.

But about four years into their stay at Schenley Gardens my dad's health began to fail and he was diagnosed with kidney failure.

He started dialysis in 2013.

Dialysis is not an easy process. He was exhausted after every treatment.

But he did it so he could stay longer with Evelyn.

He hung on for two years until his body began to break down.

When my father died, I was there with my mom, my brother, Dave and Perry in a room at UPMC – Shadyside Hospital.

Dave pushed Evelyn's wheelchair close to our dad's bed.

She reached for his hand and begged, "Paul, don't leave me."

But as much as he tried to stay with her, he slipped away, leaving the love of his life without him for the first time in nearly seven decades.

Evelyn looked at Paul and then at all of us, as if to ask us what was next and how she would live without my dad at her side.

I hugged her, pulling her close.

Honestly mom, I have no idea how to live without him, I thought.

But we'll figure it out … together.

I promise.

Chapter 3 –

The Lockdown Begins

FROM THE START, I BEGAN each new day of our quarantine by putting a line through the date on the Catholic calendar hanging next to my mom's bed.

At that point, we thought the lockdown could take us into early April, at the latest.

I knew this arrangement – having me there night and day – would be confusing for Evelyn, particularly because we wouldn't be able to venture outside, which since her stroke, she loved to do at every opportunity, even on the dreariest of days.

One thing about my girl Evelyn, she saw sunshine even through the clouds of an overcast day and I mean this literally and figuratively.

I backed up the calendar by writing on a white board tacked on another wall:

In big letters, I wrote:

"Quarantine Day 1…We can't go out — Virus"

Every morning, after crossing out the day on the calendar, I'd update the white board.

I fell into a quarantine ritual that suited us both.

Each morning, I'd also do an inventory of our snacks on the shelf beneath my parents' wedding photo.

How she loved to look at that photo and remember that day.

And how I loved to hear about it.

They were so young and so in love, a love that never waned. I know she missed him and I wished there was something I could do to fill that emptiness.

But there wasn't.

Klimovich Family photo
Evelyn and Paul Klimovich on their May 21, 1949 wedding day.

I decided early on to keep a journal of my days in lockdown with Evelyn. Along the way, I'd snap a few photos of our time together and maybe shoot a video or two.

Part of it was the journalist in me wanting to chronicle this time and maybe write a story when the quarantine was over, but I also wanted the photos to share with my brother and sisters and Perry on the outside.

I know this time was hard for them, too.

They were locked out, not knowing what was happening inside the walls of this nursing home, all while hearing the horror stories of what was playing out in other facilities across the nation where people were dying.

We are a close family and what affects one of us, affects all of us, even though miles may separate us.

Add to that the fact that our affection for our parents runs so deep. We have never taken them for granted and all they sacrificed to give us the lives we have today.

Our first full day in lockdown was a Saturday, a day when Evelyn and I normally would head out to lunch, the mall or to the casino.

Being outside energized Evelyn. She loved to be around people.

Some days, I'm not so sure she was ready to head back to the nursing home when I told her it was time to load her and her wheelchair back into the car, an all too familiar routine for her and for me.

I'd make sure the brakes were engaged on the wheelchair, then stand her up, swivel her body, place her bottom on the front seat, then lift her legs and guide them inside.

I'd buckle her seatbelt, cover her with that ubiquitous leopard print blanket and we were off, but not before collapsing her wheelchair, then hoisting it into the back of my SUV.

When we'd get back to the nursing home, we'd reverse the process, with Evelyn usually joking to someone that I'd never dropped her … yet.

I went through the process so often that I could do it in my sleep.

With my mom, I saw what a difference it made in her once we were back at the nursing home where she'd proudly tell everyone about her day out with her "Jo."

One of the people she'd always brag to was Monique Hurt-Jones, an effervescent, kind and loving nursing assistant, with whom she became particularly close.

We met Monique the first week that my mom moved to Charles Morris and the relationship just grew from there.

Monique was a gem, always making a fuss over my mom, making her feel special and always looking out for her when I wasn't there.

She understood how protective I was of Evelyn, whom she called Miss Evie.

"One couldn't live without the other," Monique said about my mom and me.

She recalled that when Evelyn first arrived at Charles Morris in 2016, "you didn't want to leave her" out of fear that something would happen to her.

"I have been working in this field since 1991 and most family members come and go a couple times a week or you see them just on holidays, but you can tell the bond you two shared was different," she said. "I figured you must have made a promise to her."

So when a lockdown became a possibility, Monique was sure of one thing.

"I knew you would be there (in quarantine) as long as Miss Evie was there," she said.

On this first full day in lockdown, Evelyn woke up about 9 a.m.

I was up and awake long before her, just looking around the room, trying to settle in for the long haul.

For just a moment, when I first woke up, I wondered whether the events of the previous day really happened.

I'd slept overnight at the nursing home before, but I'd always had the option of getting up and leaving if I wanted.

Not today.

I got Evelyn washed and dressed.

I was concerned about a rash on her chest that didn't seem to be getting any better.

I made a mental note to mention it later to someone on the staff.

Breakfast came around 9:15.

She had hot tea and a blueberry muffin. I had my Frosted Flakes.

One of the aides came around to take our temperatures, which became part of the daily drill, along with a check of our oxygen levels to ensure we weren't showing signs of "the virus."

At this point, we weren't required to wear face masks.

Evelyn and I talked while I put away some of the things I'd brought with me the night before.

She asked if we could go out and I had to tell her no.

I hoped she understood.

We were locked up – for better or worse – for 14 days, I told her.

I thought she was beginning to understand as she looked at me with her sad eyes.

We didn't talk about it again as we went about our morning, tidying up our room, changing the sheets on our beds and watching a little TV.

We watched a "Roseanne" marathon and ate peanut butter and jelly sandwiches for lunch.

Afterward, my mom looked at the white board and said: "I can't go out? And you can't go out either?"

"That's right, Mom," I said. "You can't go out and I can't go out either."

She stared at me with a puzzled look on her face.

I guess she really didn't understand.

To pass the time, we decided to work on a glow-in-the-dark jigsaw puzzle.

In sharp contrast to my "outside life" where I constantly was rushing to finish just about everything, I knew we had plenty of time to finish the puzzle later.

We were about a third of the way through when my mom asked to take a nap.

It seemed that lately, she tired so much more easily.

She was 93, after all. I guess she was entitled to a nap.

I got her into bed, tucked her in and asked if she needed anything.

She said she just wanted to rest, letting out a big sigh.

Sensing that she wanted some time alone, I decided to visit her best friend Rosie, then 96.

I walked around and snapped a picture of the empty hallway, which on normal weekends would be full of other family members on their way to visit loved ones.

On that day, you could have heard a pin drop in that hallway.

We met Rosie in September 2018.

She and my mom ate lunch and dinner together in the big, sprawling dining room at Charles Morris.

From Day 1, they clicked and I was grateful they found each other.

The long-term residents, like Rosie and my mom, had assigned seats in the dining room.

When the quarantine began, there were about 60 residents at Charles Morris, which had started limiting new-patient admissions at the start of the pandemic.

On most days, their conversation was predictable, but I think both Rosie and my mom found comfort in that.

My mother would ask Rosie, a tiny woman, if she was hungry.

Her answer was always, "no, I'm not hungry."

On the other hand, my mother was a good eater. She loved good, hearty food.

All her life, she spent time in the kitchen making big, delicious meals for our family.

Food was one way of showing her love for us.

Even though some of her foods at Charles Morris were pureed or soft so she could easily swallow them, she still had an appetite.

She and Rosie sat at the table closest to where the food was kept in warmers before it was served.

They were prime seats because their food always was nice and warm when it arrived at their table.

Many days, when I walked in the door after work, I'd find the two of them, chatting away as they finished their meals.

The first night of lockdown, I texted Rosie's son, Bobby, and daughter-in-law, Frani, and promised that I'd check on Rosie to make sure she was OK.

They all had become family to me.

We were in this together.

Bobby and Frani and I were trying our best to take care of these two women that we loved so much and Rosie, well, she became like a second mother to me.

It made me feel good to know that I was helping during this time when no one really knew what the next step was in regard to this virus.

Selfishly, I loved spending time with Rosie.

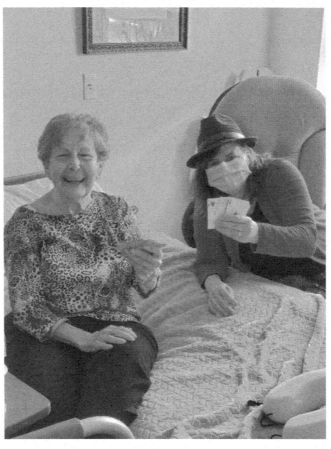

Dani Wintermyer photo
JoAnne and Rosie Wyner during one of their regular pandemic Gin Rummy games.

I always felt good after my talks with her, even on my worst days. She comforted me. She gave me her undivided attention when I was hurting, just like a mother would do. She was amazing.

She's also a talented piano player who's been playing since she was 4 and had entertained throughout Pittsburgh in her younger days.

I wrote a story about her on "Piano Day Pittsburgh" in 2019, an annual event where people are invited to play at a pre-determined destination in the city.

People gathered around her in awe of her performance at the age of 95 in downtown Pittsburgh's jam-packed Market Square where she played "Take Me Out to the Ballgame" and an assortment of Frank Sinatra numbers.

When the lunchtime crowd erupted into applause, she beamed with an ear-to-ear smile.

At Charles Morris, Rosie often entertained in the residents' lounge and television room.

Evelyn and a former resident, Matilda "Til" O'Brien, would sing along as Rosie played selections from her extensive repertoire.

It was a happy time for everyone when Rosie sat down at the piano.

But Matilda passed away in February, right before the pandemic, leaving my mom to sing alone to her friend Rosie's music.

When Matilda's daughter, Carol, heard we were quarantining, she brought us pizza and wedding soup from Mineo's Pizza House in Squirrel Hill, a favorite of ours that's known as one of the city's best spots for pizza.

Carol is another one who became like family to me.

I was with Carol and her sister, Linda, the night Matilda died. I attended her funeral. Carol gave me one of her mom's blankets – a pink one with a white pom-pom fringe.

The death of a resident also means the loss of that person's family members as your friends and confidants.

There is a huge void.

For people like my mom, it's also a reminder of their own mortality and that they're closer to the end of their lives than the beginning.

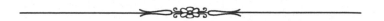

A lot of people have asked me how I was able to convince the nursing home to let me live there night and day during the largest global health crisis of our generation.

Well, it was easier than anyone might think.

It seems that the groundwork for that decision was being laid before I ever realized it.

My best answer is that my close relationship with my mother didn't go unnoticed by Debbie Winn-Horvitz, then president and CEO of the Jewish Association on Aging, which managed the nursing home.

"Everyone knew who you were, JoAnne," she told me later. "You were there all the time, and I mean that in a positive way. The relationship you had with your mom was very special. We never saw anyone coming and staying overnight with their loved one so many nights a week, so consistently, for so long."

When word of a mandatory ban on visitors was imminent, Debbie talked with her board president and then the other board members.

"I had a compassionate board president and board of directors," Debbie said. "We knew if we said 'we don't know when you can see your mom' that would not have gone over well with you. And it was not only about you. It was about the mental health and wellness of your mom. She was so used to you being there every day and being there at night. I know there were so many mornings I would be coming in (for work) and you would be walking out into the parking lot, and I would run into you."

It was a tough decision, Debbie said, because there were others who were really close with loved ones who would have loved to have been there, too.

"But we hadn't seen anyone be there in the building night after night, someone committed to being there, and not leaving as you," she said.

Debbie asked the association's attorney to draft paperwork for me to sign, freeing the home of any liability if anything happened to me.

That was the paper I signed at 5:59 p.m. on that first night.

Nothing on that paper would have changed my mind.

Truthfully, I didn't even look at it until weeks later.

During our days together, I tried to remain calm for my mom, for Rosie and for all of the residents.

It was difficult to see them alone in their rooms.

Occasional Facetime chats with family were no replacement for hugging their children and grandchildren.

I did what I could to interact with them … but safety always was an issue.

I kept my distance. I wore a mask when I was in their rooms or in the hallways.

I'd bring the woman next door towels and a nightgown every day.

I'd help some watch the numbers on their bingo cards.

I'd played cards with Rosie.

She always beat me.

As much as I tried to beat her, the woman was unstoppable.

In so many ways, she was my rock through all of this and I love her for that.

But Rosie is so easy to love.

She has such a caring nature.

I hugged her often.

I cried with her.

As time passed, she became more worried about the virus … and rightly so.

None of us knew what was next or what would happen if we got sick.

I was so grateful to have Rosie there with me. I hope that on some level, she found comfort in me.

I guess I wasn't the only one who was grateful.

One of those first nights in quarantine, Evelyn woke up around 3 a.m.

She called my name like she had so many times in the middle of the night.

I got her out of bed, into her wheelchair and rolled her into the bathroom.

Then I slid her back into bed, covered her and sat down on my cot across the room.

"JoAnne?"

"Do you need something?" I asked.

"Thank you," she said.

"Thanks for what?"

"Thank you for taking such good care of me."

Holding back tears, I said, "You're welcome."

It's just one of those early morning and late-night scenes that play over and over again in my head.

Each time, they're memories that are as vivid as when they first happened.

And each time, they make me cry.

The second full day of our quarantine was tough.

It was Sunday, always our big day together, doing the things we both loved.

The day traditionally began with Mass at St. Rosalia, the church that I grew up in, then lunch at Big Jim's, just down the street from the house on Stanley Street in Greenfield where I was raised.

Evelyn loved Big Jim's and the people there adored her.

I would call ahead to make sure it wasn't too crowded, then wheel her up the ramp into the kitchen. She would laugh because she got to see the inner workings of her favorite restaurant. The cooks and dishwasher always greeted us, often moving boxes out of the way to clear our path.

A waitress would have hot coffee, cream and sugar, and a cup of steaming Italian wedding soup ready and waiting on the first table, our favorite spot.

Big Jim's is that place where you always feel welcome.

Every Pittsburgh neighborhood has a spot like "Big Jim's."

It's a perfect fit for Greenfield.

Even though I live on the other side of the city in the suburbs, I always feel like I'm back home at Big Jim's.

There is nothing fancy about the place. The plates and cups don't match. The chairs and tables don't either.

But what it lacks in ambiance, it makes up for with warmth.

Opened in 1977, the portions are huge. The former owner, Big Jim, was a big guy, in stature and personality.

The people who work there know most of the customers by name.

They know what we like to eat and drink, especially those of us who are picky — like me.

One of the waitresses there, my friend Cindy Vandergrift, always tried to make fun of me when Evelyn and I would come into the restaurant.

Cindy understands me and she completely understood Evelyn.

She cared for her dad and her mom, who was in a wheelchair, so she has a special connection with elderly people and she'd always joke with Evelyn.

Cindy would poke fun at me, but in the end, my mom would always stick up for me and tell everybody "what a good daughter" I was to her.

Evelyn loved a good joke, especially when it wasn't at her expense.

But on that second full day of our lockdown – Sunday, March 15, 2020 – there was no Big Jim's or wedding soup for Evelyn as the world around us was slowly shutting down.

On that day, we sat in our room and Evelyn prayed the rosary as we watched our Catholic Mass at noon on TV.

I don't remember missing Mass since I was a junior at Penn State and participated in the annual THON, a dance marathon to benefit children with cancer and their families where we danced for 48 hours from 7 p.m. Friday to 7 p.m. Sunday.

And that was more than three decades earlier.

My mom has been saying the rosary most of her life. Brought up in a strict Italian Catholic family, her mother attended church several days a week and praying the rosary was something she passed down to my mother.

My sister Paula recently had given mom rosary beads blessed by Pope Francis that she picked up on a visit to Rome.

The remainder of the day was spent talking, watching old shows on TV and napping.

At this point, I was working every day, making calls from the nursing home, conducting interviews and writing stories.

One day blended into the next.

The routine was the same.

Wake up.

Eat.

TV.

Eat.

Nap.

Eat.

TV.

Sleep.

In between, there were games of bingo and prayers ... lots of prayers.

In the first week of quarantine, bingo games were in the dining room.

Bingo was my mother's favorite.

If she was napping, you'd better wake her up for bingo.

She used to play every Sunday night in the St. Rosalia church basement while my dad worked selling cards for the specials.

At Charles Morris, residents won paper money they could spend at the gift shop. We visited the store weekly and purchased snacks – everything from Little Debbie snack cakes and Mountain Dew to ice cream, none of which she should have been eating because she was a diabetic, but well ... she was 93, after all.

One day before the lockdown, close to Valentine's Day, Evelyn bought a pink stuffed pig, which she often would take to bed with her.

She loved that little pig, usually tucking it under her good arm before dozing off to sleep.

But now the gift shop was closed because of the pandemic and the bingo players had to sit six feet apart in the dining room to remain socially distanced.

Still, it was nice to get out of the room for an hour even if the pandemic was putting a bit of a crimp in their socializing.

I remember one sad-eyed resident telling me, "JoAnne, I feel like I'm in jail."

And I replied, "So do I."

As the situation with the pandemic worsened on the outside and more were sick and dying, residents eventually were forced to play bingo from their doorways because they weren't permitted in the dining room.

Social distancing was strictly enforced.

JoAnne Klimovich Harrop photo

As restrictions stemming from the pandemic increased, life revolved more and more around this 250-square-foot room.

What really kept Evelyn and me going during the pandemic were the steady deliveries of food to the front desk from friends and family – care packages that nourished our bodies and our souls.

It made us feel good to know that people outside were thinking about us, even as the world around them appeared to be going crazy.

Of course, we could order from the nursing home menu, but there was nothing like the food delivered to us from the outside.

Our first homemade meal came from my lifelong friend Jane Carr-Villella. She made us her famous meatloaf, mashed potatoes, corn, bread and cookies as well as fettuccine Alfredo for another meal.

It was heavenly.

I got to walk outside for a few minutes to get the food from her.

The air felt good on my skin and in my lungs.

I'd taken for granted something as simple as fresh air.

Perry and I stayed in contact through text messages and calls.

From our different places, we watched re-runs of Pirates baseball games, including the 1979 World Series.

It was tough being separated, but Perry understood and never questioned what I was doing or why.

Our lives fell into a schedule.

In a nursing home, under any circumstances, life often revolves around food. Maybe because when you're in there, it's not as easy to hop in the car and grab a burger or a doughnut whenever or wherever you want it. You have to wait for someone to bring it to you.

On Tuesdays, a long-time volunteer, Rona, would drop off goodies ranging from Dunkin' donuts to cheesecake.

Wednesdays were French fry day. The activities director and her assistant would bring a fryer up to our floor and make golden brown potatoes served with Heinz ketchup.

They were so good and so welcomed.

On Thursdays, Charles Morris bought lunch for the workers and one of them would bring whatever they were having to me.

Fridays were ice cream days –ooey, creamy ice cream with chocolate sauce.

An office employee would text me occasionally and she and I would meet in the stairwell, which was totally against the rules.

I felt like the music from the Pink Panther should be playing as I would sneak into the stairwell to meet my "contact."

During our surreptitious meetings, she'd hand off bags of Bachman Jax cheddar cheese curls and Utz original and honey barbecue potato chips.

It's funny how little things like French fries and cheese curls become the highlight of the day when you're cut off from the rest of the world … from your world.

One of the workers brought me a loaf of bread and peanut butter so we could have it in the room in case we didn't like the meal they were serving.

I stashed it away like it was gold bullion.

At 9 p.m., each night, we prayed the rosary.

These days, there was so much to ask God about, so much to pray about.

Most nights, I'd hear the sounds of TV shows coming from residents' rooms.

Sometimes I'd hear people laughing.

Sometimes it was crying.

Even for people like my mom who considered Charles Morris her home and made the best of every day there, this pandemic was taking a toll.

Not only were the residents cut off from their families, they were forced to keep their friends within the nursing home at arm's length to prevent any possible infection from the virus.

They ate their meals in their rooms. They spent their days and their nights in their rooms, 24 hours a day, seven days a week, with an occasional trip down the hall for a shower.

I know my mom realized she was lucky to have me there with her.

The evening news seldom delivered good news to us.

On one particular night, we learned the situation with the virus was worsening.

The World Health Organization had declared a global pandemic.

Passengers and crew sickened by the virus were stranded on cruise ships. Some were dying.

And five days after I entered Charles Morris, the first Pennsylvanian died from covid-19.

Then, Gov. Tom Wolf ordered all "non-life-sustaining businesses" to close their "physical locations" by 8 p.m. March 19 or face law enforcement action.

Inside Charles Morris, things were changing.

I was allowed to push Evelyn around the hallways as long as we both wore face masks. The workers wore masks and face shields at all times.

I was worried.

But maybe there was some goodness in the fact that Evelyn still didn't quite grasp the gravity of the situation.

She glanced out the window.

"It looks so nice out there. Can we go out?"

Once again, I had to tell her no.

It broke my heart.

"This virus is pretty bad, isn't it?" she asked.

After I got her in bed, I cried.

Going outside is what kept my mother going and I had to deny her that simplest pleasure time and again.

I feared what being locked up in this place might do to her ... and to us.

As we watched the news about that crisis and the deaths that came with it, she must have been thinking about the people she'd lost during her life.

During one of our daily conversations, she asked me if I thought we see people who have passed on before us when we die.

There were so many people I know she wanted so desperately to see again.

This was such a weighty, meaningful question, I felt like I needed to give it an equally meaningful answer.

I think I may have fallen short, but she didn't seem to mind.

I said, "I think you see the people you want to see, the people you love."

I hoped that gave her some comfort because I know how desperately she wanted to know that she would see my dad, her mother, my uncles John and Danny, my aunt Lucy and her son, Paul Jr., again someday.

To this day, I'm not sure why she asked me that question, but that night she didn't sleep well.

I pulled up the blue recliner next to her bed and held her hand the rest of the evening.

I stared out the window, wondering what was happening in the world.

After an hour, I fell asleep, still holding her hand, still wondering what was ahead for the two of us.

Chapter 4 –

The Shutdown

WHEN MY CELL PHONE RANG the afternoon of March 20, my fears about the trajectory of this virus that seemed to come from nowhere and killed without prejudice were running high.

Everything and nothing made me anxious.

I would have paced, but I had nowhere to go except this 250-square-foot room.

So, when my cell phone rang late in the day and I realized it was my then-executive editor Sue McFarland calling, I had no idea what to expect.

As she spoke, I heard nothing after she said there would be layoffs at my newspaper, and I was among the many affected.

I didn't hear the explanation Sue later told me she gave that day about how company officials hoped the layoffs would be temporary and that I could be called back to work in the future.

There was so much I didn't hear that day, so much I didn't think about.

I didn't put the pieces together that one day earlier, Gov. Tom Wolf ordered a statewide closure of all "non-life-sustaining operations," spreading fears through the business community about how long the closure would last and how those businesses would weather the loss of revenue during that time.

I didn't think about the fact that my employer was no different from those others.

From talking with Sue later, I now know that painful decisions had to be made that day and the days that came before it, decisions that no one wanted to make.

With no businesses open in the communities we serve, there was no one to buy advertising in our newspapers or on our websites and therefore no revenue with which to pay our employees or meet other expenses.

With schools closing and college and pro sports canceled, there were no games for sportswriters to cover. With just about everything else in the world at a standstill, there were fewer stories for feature writers such as me to cover.

From numerous conversations with Sue, I now understand that the most daunting part of the shutdown was not knowing how long it would last.

To protect the company and its employees' futures, cost-cutting measures had to be taken, she told me.

It wasn't just about me. It was about so many others who were hurting that day, but I didn't see it that way.

All that I could think about was that my career had come to a grinding halt.

I heard none of what Sue said and I wasn't thinking about that bigger, broader picture or the others who were affected that day.

I wish I had because it would have made the entire episode a smidge easier for me.

All that I heard was "me" and "layoff" and "effective immediately."

I'm not even sure how long we talked or when or how we said goodbye.

I'm not even sure I said goodbye.

After that, my body shut down.

I shuddered.

I don't really know that I was thinking about covid or its effects on anyone or anything except me.

I was just mad.

How could this be happening? I remember asking, "Why?"

And I don't really recall anything after that.

Was I really hearing her correctly?

"Laid off?" "Me?"

I held back tears as I pressed the button to hang up.

I stared at the phone in my hand.

I think I was in shock.

I cried so hard that Evelyn, who was sitting in her wheelchair, said "Jo, what's wrong."

I barely could get the words out.

I told her what happened.

We talked for more than an hour.

She comforted me, telling me I would find another job and that I was a good worker, and many companies would want to hire me.

"Don't worry. You won't have trouble finding a job," she said.

A mother loves you no matter what and she will always believe in you, even when you don't believe in yourself.

I wanted to scream, but I was in a nursing home, and I didn't want to scare the other residents.

It was unreal.

I was angry and hurt.

I was born to be a journalist. I truly believe that.

I love what I do.

I thought back to when I delivered newspapers as a young girl.

It was a telling sign of my career path.

I didn't know what to do with this news that suddenly, without warning, my job was gone.

I texted Perry, my siblings and a few close friends.

None of them could believe it either.

About half an hour later, I got a text from Perry that said he was in the nursing home parking lot.

I'm not sure why.

He knew he wasn't allowed in because of the pandemic.

He drove there because he knew how much the job meant to me, he said later.

He said he needed to do something, anything to help.

He was mad, too.

As the workers came in to check on us, I told them about the layoff. They tried to reassure me that everything would work out.

I wasn't so sure of that.

In my mind, I ran through all the worst scenarios.

Was my career over?

Would I ever work as a journalist again?

What kind of job would I get?

How will I ever get a job when I'm locked up in this nursing home?

I didn't sleep much that night.

I felt ill.

This is the one quarantine day I will remember for the rest of my life.

I talked with Ben Schmitt, my news editor, on Saturday morning.

He was upset for me. He tried to comfort me.

I wrote this post on Facebook:

March 21, 2020 ·

I am in tears as I write this.

After 22 and ½ years I have been laid off by the Tribune-Review. Being a journalist was my dream and thanks to then-publisher Richard Mellon Scaife, the Tribune-Review allowed me to live that dream. When I was hired in October of 1997, I was the first full-time female in the sports department. It was one of the happiest days of my life, because the Tribune-Review took a chance on me. I don't have a journalism degree and was told by my college advisor at Penn State that women aren't sportswriters, to get a business degree, which I did. But I was determined to prove him wrong.

It wasn't easy being a female sports reporter in Pittsburgh, but anything that's worth it takes perseverance.

I know I am not the most talented writer, but I have been fortunate to have had some amazing editors to help pen this chapter of my life. I know that I am, at times, emotional when covering a story, but I connect with people and see them as more than words in print or a link on a web page.

I was honored to tell every story and have met some wonderful people from my 10 years in sports to the past 12-plus as a society page, fashion and features writer – never once calling in sick.

I learned how to take some decent photos and compile videos to add some visual details to go with the words. Thanks to the talented photographers who gave me guidance to see a story in addition to telling it.

And to my colleagues who do incredible work every day.

I am not sure what tomorrow will bring. But I appreciate everyone who has read what I've written from that first story on a basketball player from Upper St. Clair to my last about a talented artist from Pittsburgh's East End and every other person in between.

Everyone has a story, and I was privileged to write about every one of them. My life has been forever changed.

Then came more tears.

I was so overwhelmed by the response to my posting about my job loss. The attention to that posting helped with my pain.

The Trib sent paperwork for me to sign, and I began the process of filing for unemployment like millions of other people throughout the country, including some of my colleagues.

I felt that everything in my life was out of control.

I had only held two professional jobs in my entire life – at the Trib for 23 years and my sales job for 10 before that.

My plan was to retire from the Trib.

I began to focus on going online for unemployment benefits and coordinating the return of my computer and other company property, which included my phone.

I went through my files and saved photos and other important documents.

The devastating effects of the pandemic on the local economy had now shaken my world to its core.

I stared out the window for hours, thinking about what my next move should be.

My work computer sat on the floor. I had no use for it now.

I was crushed.

When I was hired at the Trib, I was overjoyed.

It was a dream come true.

Losing it all was my worst nightmare.

On the night of my layoff, I finally composed myself and went out to visit Rosie. She always had such a calming effect on me.

It was later than usual. She told me she was going to call my cell phone because she hadn't seen me. I didn't want to go to see her when I was so upset.

I told her about losing my job.

She gave me a hug and said she was sorry this happened.

Despite my best efforts to be strong, I cried even more.

When I thought I couldn't cry anymore, the tears would come again.

I wanted to stop, but I couldn't.

She wanted to play cards to distract me.

Rosie often played cards with her son and daughter-in-law.

Her mind is sharp and the scouting report on her around the nursing home was that despite her diminutive frame and soft-spoken nature, she was a force to be reckoned with when it came to playing cards.

I guess I realized she was more than a casual player when I noticed she had her own card shuffling machine.

Over the next day or so, the loss of my job became more and more real, and my mood moved between anger and deep sadness.

I wanted to see my friends back at the office. I'd never even had a chance to say goodbye.

For more than two decades, I'd seen them every day and I guess I took it all for granted that I'd see them the next day and the next.

I wanted to go sit at my desk in the newsroom.

I wondered what would happen to my desk and everything in it – my family photos, my mirror, my tape dispenser in the shape of a stiletto shoe, the sweater on the back of my chair, the little space heater that kept me warm in the winter and the calendar with the last day I worked – March 13 – crossed off.

In the drawers, amid the stacks of random papers, newspaper clippings and pens, were my favorite chocolates.

I wanted to smell that ever-present aroma of coffee wafting from our newsroom lounge and be tempted by the doughnuts and bagels that seemed to come from nowhere on so many days and fueled us when there was no time for real food.

I missed it all and I wanted it back.

My breaking point came on the day that my company phone was cut off.

It was enough to set me off.

I lost it … this had been one of the worst times of my life.

I took this layoff personally.

"Nearly 23 years, and they do this to me," I thought, not realizing until later that the same thing probably happened to all of the others who were laid off.

I guess I didn't think about those other people at the time.

But I'm sure they were hurting just as much as I was.

At this moment, all that I could think about was the pain and sense of betrayal that I was feeling.

Perry bought me a new phone.

People had been asking me how I was doing, and I would reply, "not good," and they would say, "Why?"

"Why do you think?" I felt like saying.

"I just lost my job of nearly 23 years, and I am in quarantine in a nursing home where I can't leave the unit …. and my 93-year-old mother isn't feeling well…sooooooooooo, how do you think I feel?"

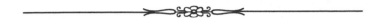

I tried to pull myself together for my mother's sake to move forward and try to observe a few of the time-honored rituals of our lives together.

Thursday, April 2 was supposed to be Opening Day for Pittsburgh Pirates baseball.

Evelyn loved her Pittsburgh sports teams, but the Pirates were her favorite.

Even when they were losing, she would say, "they are the only team we have."

There's nothing she loved better than an afternoon at the ballpark and all that came with it – the crowd, the excitement and of course, the hotdogs.

The opener was canceled because of the pandemic, but she and I dressed for the day – Evelyn in her game jersey and me in my Pirates T-shirt – and sang "Take Me Out to The Ballgame" with some of the residents and Rosie on the piano.

My mom knew every word. I recorded some video on my iPhone and played it back often. It always made me smile.

It was a great day and for that short time I forgot about my troubles.

The next day, on April 3, just two weeks after the layoff, I saw a Facebook message pop up.

It was from Jennifer Bertetto, the president of my company.

She asked me to give her a call.

I was scared to dial her number. I asked my mom what she thought I should do.

She said, "Call and see what she wants."

Just about then, Perry brought us Mineo's pizza and wedding soup.

He was always bringing us food, always checking on us to see if we needed anything. He was so good to us.

I decided to call the president after dinner.

I took a deep breath and dialed the phone.

She'd read my Facebook post.

She asked how I was doing. She asked how my mom was doing.

I cried as I told her about the quarantine and how bad things were for me.

Not long after we hung up, she sent me a message that read, "I'll see you on the other side of this pandemic. Please relax and enjoy your time with your mom. Our story together isn't over."

This buoyed my spirits.

Jennifer had met my mother at an event at the National Aviary on Pittsburgh's North Side, where she serves on the board. She saw my connection to Evelyn as I pushed her so she could see some of the birds and sample a few of the hundreds of cookies there that night.

I kept thinking about her call.

This is unbelievable. How many company presidents would reach out to an employee that they just laid off? And in the middle of a pandemic?

She cares about her people, and it shows.

The 14 days that I thought the quarantine would last had come and gone.

It dawned on me that the Easter holidays were fast approaching.

Palm Sunday, Good Friday, and Easter Sunday were all important religious holidays for us, and I needed to make sure that we observed them in an appropriate way.

Of course, that was a tall order since we were living in a Jewish-run nursing home.

But for Palm Sunday, the activities director and her assistant came through for us, bringing us homemade "palms" they fashioned from some greenery they found outside.

I hung them above a cross in my mom's room.

They'll never know how much that gesture meant to us.

When Palm Sunday finally arrived on April 5 – Day 24 of our quarantine – we were up at 9:30.

Monique brought us chicken noodle soup and cheeseburgers with fries from Eat 'n Park.

We watched Palm Sunday Mass on TV.

I wheeled my mom down the hall to see Rosie – socially distanced, of course.

They waved to each other from across the room and smiled.

They always seemed happy when they were together.

And then we sat by a window at the end of the hall.

Evelyn asked, "It looks nice outside, can we go out?"

I almost cried.

"No, mom, we can't go out."

I gazed out the window wondering when the day would come when we could venture outside the walls of this building again, when I would be able to answer by saying, "yes mom, it is a nice day, and we can go outside."

That same day, I received a text message from Rosie's daughter-in-law, Frani.

She asked if I could bring Rosie downstairs near the door so they could see her.

I inquired with the staff but was told it wasn't permitted.

I felt awful.

Rosie and her family had done so much for me, and I couldn't do this one small thing for them.

But I did help Rosie see her family on a virtual call.

It was a new world of virtual communication for all of us.

One of her relatives asked, "Who is this JoAnne on our call?"

I chuckled, explaining that because I set up the call for Rosie on my computer, my name appeared on the screen along with all of her family members.

Rosie was happy to see everyone on the computer, but knowing Rosie, what she really wanted was to be there in person with the people she loves.

As each family member's face appeared on the screen, she lovingly reached out to touch them.

When they began talking to her, a broad smile stretched across her face.

How sad that our circumstances had reduced this warm, loving woman's connection to her family to her hand touching a piece of tempered glass.

Even so, it made me happy to give Rosie this moment with her family. I only wished it could have been more.

I couldn't wait to tell Evelyn about Rosie's call, but when I returned to her room later, something wasn't quite right with her.

Waking up from a nap, she seemed confused.

Often, it would take her a little time to regain her focus after sleeping, but today was different.

She looked at me with a puzzled stare and asked why I was there.

I was shocked, but tried to answer her in my calmest voice.

I told her that I wanted to be with her during the quarantine and I said, "Isn't that nice you have me here?"

She stared back at me for a moment before replying, "It's fantastic… and you have me here, too.

"Yes, mom, it's fantastic. I have you here, too."

The next Sunday, April 12, was the first time either of us had ever missed Easter Sunday with family.

It was an odd feeling, but we tried to make the best of it.

We got up early, got dressed in our Sunday best, had breakfast and waited for the time we had set for our family's virtual call.

Evelyn was still amazed by the concept of being able to talk to everyone at the same time on the computer, but it seemed to make her happy.

Everyone talked about their lives, their families, their plans for the day and how they were navigating the pandemic.

We signed off with Evelyn waving goodbye to everyone and telling them she loved them.

After that, it was time to watch Easter Mass on TV.

While we appreciated being able to watch Mass, it just wasn't as uplifting as being there in our church on Easter Sunday and hearing the message delivered by our priest, seeing the beautiful flowers and the magnificent and powerful voices of the choir.

On any day, I drew strength from attending Mass, but these days, I leaned on my faith to get me through what seemed to be the daily challenges of this pandemic.

The remainder of the day was just like any other day.

Someone was nice enough to bring us some ham for dinner, which of course, we weren't going to get in our Jewish nursing home.

After dinner, I headed down the hall to play cards with Rosie, determined that one of these days, I would beat her.

I lost again.

I just can't stop her.

She's a shark.

Even at my age, I still look forward to my share of Easter candy.

And on this Easter, it was my friend, Jane, to the rescue with chocolate and Mountain Dew.

I couldn't imagine not having candy on Easter, particularly this year.

After giving up chocolate for Lent, even as an adult, I was always the one who tore into my chocolate bunny on Easter morning, eating the ears before anything else.

I didn't have a bunny this year, but that chocolate that Jane brought for me was so good.

I sat back and savored every bite.

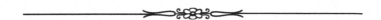

On April 16, our 35th day in quarantine, my phone rang again with a call from Sue, my executive editor.

After almost three weeks, the sting of losing my job was still fresh, but I was learning to live with it.

I took Sue's call and I'm glad I did because she was calling to ask me to come back to work. I couldn't believe what I was hearing.

This time, I listened as she spoke.

She was happy and so was I.

She reminded me that she'd told me in our first call that she'd hoped to recall me.

I told her that I had no recollection of her saying that.

Suddenly, a flood of new emotions overcame me.

I was ecstatic, but worried about how I would do the work.

Could I do a good job while locked up inside this nursing home?

I knew in my heart that my mom's health was quickly deteriorating.

In the prior weeks, we'd seen several doctors for a number of tests trying to figure out what was wrong with Evelyn.

The news was not good.

Since then, she'd spent a lot of time sleeping and had little appetite.

When Sue called, she asked how my mom was doing and I told her.

She assured me that while everyone else on the staff was still working from home, I could work from the nursing home, and everything would be OK.

She said the company would help me work out a schedule while I was still in quarantine.

Despite all of that, I was anxious beyond words.

But my mom and the workers were happy I got my job back.

The housekeeper, Carol, brought me pizza to celebrate.

She has always been such a positive, upbeat presence for everyone around her.

She not only did her job well, but she looked out for the residents and now, she looked out for me.

April 20, my first day back at work, was a great day.

I created a little workspace in the corner of the room with a chair and my tray table. I booted up my computer, checked my email and read the Trib online.

I was used to writing and doing interviews in that noisy newsroom, so I was certain I could make this work.

I contacted my news editor, Ben, and talked about my assignments for the day.

Normally, I'd be out in the field doing in-person interviews for stories that I'd write, but the Trib was permitting me to stick with stories that could be completed by phone or by Zoom, Teams or whatever video-conferencing program the subject of my interviews happened to be using.

So much of the world's work was being done remotely, so I didn't feel like I was missing much.

It felt good to be working. It also kept my mind off whatever was happening with my mom's health.

The thing I love about journalism is meeting new people.

I try to do everything I can to make them feel comfortable about talking with me, about sharing personal information. I've found that it often helps to tell them something about me to make them feel more comfortable about opening up about themselves.

I try to make every story the most important one I have ever written, because it is to the person I am interviewing.

This is what I missed most during my layoff.

Often, when I would be interviewing sources for a story during the pandemic, it would come up that I was conducting the interviews from a nursing home where I was quarantining with my mother.

That certainly was a conversation starter.

The next day I did a few phone interviews, but I kept running into dead ends.

When my editor asked about the status of a story that was assigned to me, I told him that I'd made some calls about it, but no one was calling me back.

I hated telling him that, but there was nothing I could do about it.

Normally, when then happened, I'd just jump in my car and track down the subject for the interview, but that wasn't happening.

I was feeling a little frustrated.

If I left the building, I couldn't return, so there was no way I was leaving.

And so, I stayed and made the best of the situation I was in. It's all that I could do.

In doing interviews for this book, I've asked a lot of people if they ever doubted that I would make it through the entire lockdown with my mother.

For the most part, they all said they knew that I would hang in there with Evelyn for as long as the quarantine was in place.

"I know you love your job, but you love your mother more," my sister Ruth said. "We are all really glad she had you there. She would have been in there all alone and scared and she didn't understand what was going on.

"That is the kind of determination you have. You say 'this is what I am going to do' without thinking about the 'what ifs'. You stick to your decisions. I wish I was like that."

Chapter 5 –

Perry

MY HUSBAND PERRY GETS ME.

When the rest of world looks at me with baffled astonishment, he understands me.

He's a calming influence when life throws a wrench in the works.

He brings order to my frequent chaos.

And that certainly was the case in the spring of 2020 when a global pandemic sent us and the rest of the world into a lockdown.

We were barely 18 when we met more than four decades ago in college in the midst of an academic crisis – mine, not his.

We both started college in 1981 at what was then known as Penn State – McKeesport, a tiny branch campus with just one dorm.

Just 12 miles down the Monongahela River from Pittsburgh, set amid a number of gritty, working-class Mon Valley towns decimated by the collapse

of the region's steel industry in the early 1980s, the school wasn't glamorous, but it immediately felt like home to me.

A year earlier, if you'd told me I'd be at Penn State-McKeesport, I would have laughed at you.

You see, from an early age, I had a master plan for my life, and it didn't include the Mon Valley or Penn State.

But I now believe that there was another plan put in place by a higher power and my stay at Penn State was an integral part of it.

Without it, there would have been no Perry in my life.

Without it, I might not have been in Pittsburgh to take care of my parents when they needed me most.

I shudder to think of where life might have taken me without Penn State and without Perry.

Somehow my parents scraped together the money to send us all to Catholic schools with the exception of the twins, who went to the Pittsburgh Public Schools for high school.

So, it was only natural that I planned to continue my Catholic education at the University of Notre Dame.

But apparently no one told the powers-that-be at Notre Dame.

When I wasn't accepted, I needed a Plan B, and I needed it quickly.

I didn't want to attend the University of Pittsburgh, which I could almost see from my parents' house. That was just too close to home.

Duquesne University, just a smidge farther down the road, was a great Catholic school, but way too expensive.

I wasn't accepted to the main campus of Penn State, so I thought I'd go to the McKeesport branch for two years then transfer to the main campus my junior year.

Even so, I knew I was going to have to pay for my education with grants and loans because my parents just didn't have the means to do it.

Money was tight for me freshman year, so I managed to get a work-study job checking in students for meals in the cafeteria.

That's where I first saw Perry.

Tall and thin with sandy brown hair, I thought he was nice looking, but I was too caught up in adjusting to college life to think about him much more than just the "guy from the cafeteria" who smiled as he passed by me each day with his buddies.

I was friendly to him, but that was it.

I actually only knew him by the number on his dining card. My entire freshman year, I never even knew his name.

It wasn't until my sophomore year that I really got to know him.

That's also when I decided I might flunk accounting unless I could find someone to help me.

A logical question would be why a would-be journalist, let alone an aspiring sportswriter such as myself, was taking accounting.

Well, back then, in some academic circles, it seemed unthinkable and even foolish to encourage a woman to become a sportswriter even though women were beginning to make some inroads in the profession.

Women were advised to pursue studies leading to more traditional roles in sales, marketing or finance.

My adviser suggested a business degree and I heeded his advice.

It was decidedly poor judgment on my part.

But that's what led me to accounting and what led my roommate, Tracey Nicholas, and me to search the only dorm on campus for this nameless guy from the cafeteria, whom by then I recognized as a standout student from my accounting class.

Surely, he could help me if only we could find him, I thought.

We started knocking on doors in the male section of our three-story dorm.

Finally, on the second floor, he opened the door.

Paydirt.

Tracey pushed me into his room, handed him the thick Accounting 101 textbook and said, "help my roommate with accounting. She really needs help."

He looked stunned.

I looked relieved, Tracey later told me.

Without any hesitation, this guy who I quickly learned was named Perry Harrop, began patiently tutoring me a few days a week.

I struggled with balance sheets, expenses and assets, capital and cash flow. Truth be told, I struggled with just about every aspect of accounting.

I think he might have been amused by how inept I was at something that came so easily to him.

He'd stay up late trying to help, reviewing the same concepts over and over again.

He was an accounting whiz and accounting clearly would not be my life's work.

I would bring him brown sugar cinnamon Pop Tarts for payment.

I memorized enough to pass the class. To this day, I'm not good with numbers.

"In college, for a guy, food was a good motivator, so that's how we started," Perry said.

Eventually, he would ask for help editing papers for his business writing class.

We started to grow closer, and our personalities just clicked.

"JoAnne was very personable, and everybody liked her, and everyone wanted to be around her," Perry recalled about their college days. "She was engaging and upbeat."

Tracey, who now lives in North Carolina, said she remembers searching the dorm that day for Perry – whom for some inexplicable reason she lovingly calls "Percy" to this day.

She was determined to find him because she saw how much I was struggling with my accounting class.

She was such a good friend and remains so today.

Back then, we called ourselves Ebony and Ivory because Tracey is Black, and I am white. We became fast friends from day one, sharing all that came with our new lives as college students.

It's funny, but back then, we thought we were just about the coolest girls at Penn State-McKeesport, partly because we were recognized with an award for being the "best roommates" on campus that year.

We loved the recognition. We loved just about everything about being at McKeesport.

Even then, Tracey said she knew there was something special about my relationship with Perry.

And Perry and I knew it, too.

"God gave you the perfect person in Percy," Tracey said. "Percy was supposed to be the accounting guy, but he ended up being THE guy."

Tracey, like Perry, noticed my connection to my parents.

"I saw the way they loved you," Tracey said. "They poured everything into you. What you and your parents had was grounded in cement. They loved how Perry loves you, and he understood the depth of your love for them. Your parents made it easy to be around them and to love them. They put everything into you, and you gave it all back."

My first real date with Perry was at the Pizza Hut in McKeesport.

We walked the three-mile round trip because neither of us had a car.

But it didn't matter where we were headed or how we got there.

It was just being together that was important. We were young and all of this relationship stuff was brand new to us, but looking back, we should have known that something special was happening.

Our conversations were easy, like we'd known each other for years, not months.

He loved sports and so did I, so we had that common ground.

But the connection went beyond that. There was a comfort and ease about our relationship that always made me feel safe.

Our second date was a game of basketball, called H-O-R-S-E, which I won, although Perry may have had a few drinks, which could have affected his ability to make some of the baskets.

Basketball was a shared passion. I played in high school. I stress that I played. I didn't say that I played well.

And Perry lived and breathed basketball.

And so, our relationship grew from there.

Those were great years at McKeesport.

That year, I decided to travel to Penn State's main campus to take part in its giant charity dance marathon, and Perry stepped in to save the day when I arrived home after dancing nonstop for 48 hours.

It was mentally grueling, but also took an emotional toll.

There were a few times I wanted to quit, but my parents taught us to finish what we started, and they were in the audience, so quitting was not an option.

About halfway through the event, the organizers brought in some of the young cancer patients benefiting from the marathon and that made me cry, but it energized me as well and I kept going.

These kids were the ones facing challenges, not me.

By the time my parents dropped me off at my dorm, I was exhausted, and my legs were so stiff from being stuffed in the back seat of their car for 2 ½ hours, I couldn't walk.

Perry appeared out of the blue and carried me back to my room.

"I remember your mom saying, 'I hope he doesn't drop her,'" Perry said.

He didn't.

I could have never known at that moment how many times – both literally and figuratively – I would need Perry to carry me.

We knew the day would come when we both would have to leave the comfort and security of our lives at our branch campus and move to the main campus for our junior and senior years.

For Perry, the main campus, with its miles of tree-lined streets and tens of thousands of students, was exciting.

For me, it was painfully overwhelming and impersonal.

Perry jumped right into life at Penn State, living on campus, making friends and soaking up the big college atmosphere, the excitement of football weekends in the era of Joe Paterno and the feeling of being part of the much-heralded Penn State tradition.

For me, Penn State was so enormous that just getting from place to place was beyond daunting.

I lived off campus with friends who also made the move from McKeesport, but I never really felt the bond with the school that most people feel and that stayed with me until the day I graduated.

I just felt so disconnected from everyone and everything that I couldn't wait to leave there at the end of many weeks to head home to Pittsburgh.

Back home in Greenfield is where I wanted to be.

Perry thought it was odd that I'd jump at any opportunity to leave Penn State on the weekends and return to Greenfield, leaving the excitement of Penn State football and college life behind.

For most students, Saturdays were all about football games and tailgating with friends.

"She missed half of the football games, and I would be thinking 'Why would you want to miss a football game?'" he said. "But I realized how important her family was to her and any time she could be with them, she would go."

I did go home a lot. I wanted to see my parents. If you grow up in Greenfield, it's always part of you. I always felt comfortable there. I still do.

I liked going to a couple of football games. but I didn't feel like I was missing anything if I wasn't there. If there was a game at 3:30, I didn't feel like I wanted to show up and start drinking at 9 a.m.

Truthfully, if it hadn't been for our time at McKeesport and that accounting class, Perry and I might have never met. I am a true believer that we meet people in our lives for a reason at a specific time.

Some stay for a short time.

Others become a part of our lives forever.

They are part of our life story.

That's Perry.

Perry met my family – my entire family – for the first time in the summer of 1985.

Up to that point, he'd met my parents, but that was it.

But this time, everyone was there because my grandmother, Maddalena, was visiting from Florida, where she'd moved in 1958.

Her trips back to Pennsylvania were monumental reasons to celebrate for our family.

She was the reason that a lot of us exist today. She was the woman who held the family together when it could have fallen to pieces in an instant.

There were brothers, sisters, aunts, uncles, nieces, nephews all crammed into my parents' tiny house in Greenfield.

There were mounds of food everywhere and simultaneous, boisterous conversations happening all around Perry.

When he arrived there that day it was quite a scene. There were people everywhere. There was nowhere to sit. People were piled up on couches, which was totally normal for us, but I am sure he was wondering what was going on. He told me later that he could tell how close our family was just by the way everyone acted that day.

It was quite a departure from his much quieter, small family with just his parents and his younger brother, Todd, who all moved to Pittsburgh when Perry was in sixth grade and Todd was in fifth.

At the Klimovich house, there were loads of people who wanted to meet him.

The older women hugged him.

The men shook his hand.

There were slaps on the back and serious conversations with this new person who was, on this day, for all intents and purposes, "applying for entry" into this large and loving family.

Perry loved it all.

By the end of the day, Grandma gave him the thumbs up.

Perry was in.

He was part of the family.

Later in 1985, graduation finally rolled around, and it was time to leave school, get a job and begin our lives.

Perry and I hadn't talked about getting married at that point, but we talked about how we would stay together as we moved on from Penn State.

It was assumed that I would move back to Pittsburgh.

There never was any question about that.

I took a job with a company called Friden Alcatel selling machines that stamped envelopes with a red impression that replaced postage stamps.

Pitney Bowes was the top seller of these mailing machines. Friden Alcatel was second.

Although I tried to approach the job with enthusiasm, I knew I wasn't building a career with this company.

It wasn't my dream job. It was a job that offered me a paycheck every two weeks. Period.

Perry had done an accounting internship with Deloitte Haskins and Sells in New York City's World Trade Center and was offered a job there after graduation.

We decided that at least temporarily ours would be a long-distance relationship.

I flew at least once a month to visit him on People Express — a popular low-cost airline that required you to pay for your ticket in flight. It was an exciting time for us, living in two places, spending time in New York, trying to figure out our future and our careers. At the same time, it was unsettling, not knowing what the future held for us.

Our weekends together were wonderful, but then came Sundays when I had to pack up to leave.

Inevitably, I would be sitting on the plane home sobbing about the fact that I had to leave, knowing that I wouldn't see Perry again for several more weeks. I really didn't know how much longer I could do this.

In between the visits, we exchanged cards and letters updating each other about our weeks, our feelings for each other, our hopes for the future and our frustrations with our jobs.

Back then, people still wrote letters. I miss those days.

In reality, Perry always sent me cards and letters, even back at Penn State – McKeesport when we were living in the same building.

I saved each of those letters, some funny, some poignant, all displaying a degree of love and devotion that I'd never known.

Almost all of his letters start, with, "I love you" and end with, "Love you forever, Perry."

All of his letters talked about how much he missed me.

And I missed him, but I didn't see any immediate end in sight to our long-distance relationship.

Though Perry was in a much-sought-after position with a top-flight company, neither one of us was happy in our jobs.

He hated the stress and the incredibly long, exhausting hours expected of young associates in his company.

In the back of my mind, I knew that I wanted to be a journalist.

Our mission was clear.

We needed to live in the same city, and we needed to find work that meant more than just a regular paycheck.

In 1986, Perry made part of our dream become reality when he transferred from New York to the Pittsburgh office of Deloitte Haskins and Sells.

Life became a little less hectic in those days and we found comfort in being in the same city, seeing each other on a regular basis.

In Perry's mind, the next step was obvious.

In July 1987, he devised a plan to ask me to marry him.

So much thought went into it. He wanted it to be perfect.

There would be dinner and a romantic proposal.

But of course, I threw a wrench in the works.

I called to tell him I couldn't see him that night. I had a work emergency.

A customer needed extra training on a machine so that's where I'd spend my night.

Perry, who'd walked around with the engagement ring in his pocket for days, quickly switched gears.

He hatched a Plan B to propose the next day while we were eating lunch at a picturesque, glass-enclosed courtyard dotted with tables and chairs at PPG Plaza in downtown Pittsburgh.

It wasn't the romantic setting that he'd planned for the night before, but it would work.

We met there often on weekdays to order some lunch from a nearby food court and eat outside before heading back to work.

So right there, just after we finished eating, he got down on one knee, in front of the plaza's lunchtime crowd and asked me to marry him.

I had no clue this was coming and I know my eyes nearly popped from my head as he pulled the ring from his pocket.

I'm not sure if people around us noticed what was going on or even if anyone acknowledged us.

In that moment, it was just us.

I was surprised … really surprised. "Yes!" I told him, as we hugged, still oblivious to the people around us.

It wasn't a romantic dinner, but his proposal was perfect and when I recount the details, I can remember it all like it was yesterday.

Perry later told me he knew the proposal had to happen then. He couldn't wait any longer. It was one of the few moments that I've known him to truly be nervous about anything. He's usually the calmest person in the room. But not on that day.

He later told me he was sweating with that ring in his pocket and probably wasn't thinking as romantically as he wanted to be, but he just needed to get the words out of his mouth and get that ring on my finger.

If I'd only had some inkling of what he was planning, I probably would have made it easier on the poor guy and tried a little harder to make it to that romantic dinner after dealing with my customer's crisis.

The ring was beautiful. I had no input into selecting it, but it was perfect.

The celebration that day was short-lived because Perry had to hurry back to his office, leaving me there alone in the courtyard to stare at my new ring and process this information.

I am getting married, I thought to myself over and over.

I had one of those clunky old bag cell phones that I used to call my parents and give them the good news. They were elated.

My mom said, "you better come over here so we can talk all about this."

She was excited for me and for Perry and about the thought of planning a wedding.

I wasn't their first daughter to get married – two of my three sisters were married – but I was their baby, and I was about to walk down the aisle.

That Sunday, we all got together, and the wedding planning began. My parents were so thrilled for us, and although they didn't have the money in the bank to pay for our wedding, they borrowed from their credit union to foot the bill, much the same as they had for the other family weddings.

We were married Sept. 3, 1988, at St. Rosalia Church in Greenfield with a reception at the Sharpsburg Fire Hall for 200 guests.

That's what we did back then in Greenfield – a good old-fashioned fire hall wedding with lots of guests. I wouldn't have had it any other way.

The rain held off until later in the day, so our wedding party didn't get drenched going to or from the church.

The girls in the wedding – my three sisters, a friend from college, Denise, and my Greenfield friend – my very first friend ever – Therese, my maid of honor, all wore bright red dresses with puffy sleeves, and the guys wore dark gray tuxes with red bowties and red cummerbunds, including Perry's brother Todd, who was best man.

Those big puffy dresses were all the rage back then.

It was a raucous Greenfield neighborhood party with one of the highlights of the night being "the cup dance" in which guests crush Styrofoam cups while dancing.

Each person tries to find a unique way to do it.

I rolled over the cup in my mermaid-style wedding dress before Perry took his turn in his tux.

Everyone did it.

It's a Greenfield thing.

We went to Walt Disney World on our honeymoon, but it was anything but relaxing. A hurricane swept through Florida, sending flood waters gushing through the streets of Orlando.

The winds were terrible, and the water was up to our knees.

People who lived there talked about how this was the worst storm they'd ever seen.

I cried.

It was awful and I wanted to leave.

I told Perry, "Take me back to Greenfield!"

Perry freely admits that marrying me has changed his view of the world.

"I am a lot better person because of JoAnne. I am more empathetic because of her," he said.

From a practical standpoint, Perry has made me more financially responsible.

I haven't always been that way.

When we first got together, he'd help me with my taxes and of course, I had no records of anything and he'd tell me, "No, no, no you have to have receipts!"

He doesn't scream. He doesn't yell. He always assumes that things will work out. When there's a problem, he calmly works through it until we find a solution.

I guess you could say that Perry got a second set of parents when he married me.

When his parents moved to Georgia, and then to their current home in Florida, my mom and dad treated him like one of their own.

My mom loved to take care of people and with Perry's parents so far away, she saw an opportunity to be there for him and support him.

In 1989, he saw an ad for a grade school basketball coach at St. Rosalia School in Greenfield, my alma mater.

When he got the job, my mom became his No. 1 fan.

And when he moved on to coach at the high school level, her support continued, as did mine.

I noticed his dedication to the sport when we were in college.

He was the game announcer for the Penn State-McKeesport men's team and would work out with the squad.

He was at home on the court.

It made him happy in the same way that writing satisfied me.

By the mid-1990s, I was beginning to feel really restless in my job.

So, I decided to leave that job and chase my dream of becoming a sportswriter. It was the summer of 1995.

Perry was my cheerleader.

When others told me how difficult it would be to make this move, he never doubted me.

When I reached out to the Trib and another Pittsburgh paper multiple times a month, I was turned away each time because I had no experience.

As I tried to get that experience, I earned a little money writing for weekly and monthly newspapers, covering school board and council meetings and cranking out features stories – just so I could build a portfolio of work to show prospective employers.

One of those publications was the monthly Greenfield Grapevine.

I was so proud to tell the stories of the people in the neighborhood where I grew up. I wrote for free just to get some experience.

It was a wild ride that lasted two years.

I bugged the high school sports editor at the Trib over and over again until he threw me some crumbs and let me cover a few high school tennis matches and a feature about a local high school basketball player as a freelancer.

One day, he asked me to cover some power boat races at the annual regatta in downtown Pittsburgh.

After I agreed to cover the races, one of the other editors said, "You know, they usually crash."

I looked at him thinking, "I'm covering the race, not a wreck."

Well, he was right.

Two of the boats, which can travel 100-miles-per-hour or more, collided. A driver was taken to nearby Allegheny General Hospital.

There were no cell phone photos at that time, so I grabbed film from spectators and told them I'd pay to have it developed for them if they'd let us use it.

Later, I was assigned to cover the annual Family House polo match at Hartwood Acres, a beautiful, sprawling 600-acre park with a mansion and a network of lush walking, hiking and bridle paths, just north of the city.

It seemed like such an innocuous assignment.

Polo seemed so refined.

What could go wrong?

I found out the next day when a player was murdered overnight by his girlfriend, and it just so happened that I had interviewed the woman prior to the match and the polo player after his team won.

I heard about the murder from my mom, who'd seen it on the TV news.

Since she knew I had covered the event, she wanted to clue me in on the latest development.

Sometimes Evelyn was my best source out there in the community. She was a great news hound in addition to being a great mother.

The Trib's police reporter helped fill in the holes and the story made the front page.

As a freelance writer, having your story appear on page 1 is rewarding beyond description.

The Trib editor who warned me about the possible power boat crash gave me the nickname "Scoop" because I nailed down the story.

Although I was offered a full-time position as a news reporter, I turned it down.

I told the editor who offered me the job, "Thanks, but no, I really want to be a sportswriter."

He said he might have a position available in a few months.

I said," I'll wait."

He called two months later and offered me a job in sports.

I was hired on Oct. 14, 1997.

Perry and I celebrated.

I didn't even ask what the salary was or how much vacation I would get or even what sports I would be covering.

I just said, "Yes."

A decade after I made the switch to journalism, it was Perry's turn to make a similar bold move, leaving the accounting world to take a job teaching high school students 'financial literacy" at City Charter High School and coaching basketball.

It's a job that he loves, doing what he loves, working with kids and coaching.

His proudest days were those when he was head coach at Northgate in Evelyn's hometown of Bellevue.

I always knew it was a change he had to make.

Each time we made a career change, it had a financial impact on our lives for a while, but we weren't worried about it.

The good thing was that we made those career changes at different times.

And we were both finally doing work that we were meant to do.

Perry and I both have sports in our blood.

Although I made the switch from sports to features after some cajoling and a bit of a financial incentive by a former executive editor, I still miss the thrill of covering sports.

I come from a sports family, which was one of the things that Perry noticed about me when we first met.

A big night for my family was gathering in the living room to watch sports – just about any kind of sports – on television.

My parents' favorite was Pirates baseball games, sometimes watching the same one twice – once live in the afternoon and then the rerun of the game later that same evening.

Perry and I would golf with my dad on Father's Day and on his birthday.

A highlight for Perry and me was visiting the Basketball Hall of Fame when we traveled to Massachusetts for a Greenfield neighbor's wedding.

I took my parents to some of the high school playoff games Perry coached. I swear they cheered for him and his team until they were hoarse and then cheered some more.

He and my mom attended a Pittsburgh Pirates playoff game. It was a magical moment for her that she never forgot.

When Perry coached basketball at St. Rosalia, Evelyn would work dinner around his games and his practices. When it was cold outside, she'd make him bring his basketballs into the house so they wouldn't lose air. That always made them both laugh.

Perry tells everyone that he was so lucky because Paul and Evelyn treated him just like one of their kids.

He loved them and they loved him back with all their heart. So, when the subject of my mom's nursing home being locked down at the start of the pandemic came up, no real discussion was needed.

"It was automatic," Perry said. "There wasn't any conflict about it. I just knew. I knew that was what she would want to do. Of course, we didn't know how long it would last."

No, we didn't. We thought it would be two weeks.

Most people did.

And most people, including Perry and me, were wrong.

Chapter 6 –

Bad News Just Keeps Coming

THOUGH I WANTED TO DENY it, I knew in my heart that something was seriously wrong with Evelyn.

I didn't need medical tests or doctors to tell me that she was slowly but surely slipping away from me.

In what seemed like just a couple of weeks she'd become frail and weak, sleeping most of the day, barely lifting her head some days to take only a bite or two of the cookies and cakes she once gobbled up like there was no tomorrow.

The weight dropped at an alarming rate from her already tiny frame and her eyes showed a degree of surrender I'd never seen before.

The rash on her chest that I noticed just before the start of the pandemic was spreading, digging more deeply into her paper-thin skin despite an antibiotic that she was on for several days.

Getting to the root of what was happening to her became my obsession.

Some days the burden of that obsession became overwhelming.

Seeing the pain in her eyes day after day, it was all that I could think about.

There was no respite from it. It was with me night and day because I was there with her night and day.

If there was ever a time in my life when I needed to do the right thing, this was it, I told myself.

But the pandemic kept getting in my way.

A mammogram the doctor ordered was canceled because of the pandemic.

No surprise there. The world outside was awash in fear about the virus.

Medical appointments for anything less than emergencies were canceled or rescheduled as virtual appointments.

At that point, I wasn't calling the shots, which made me feel incapable, inadequate and helpless.

I knew I could do better for my mother if I could just get her in front of a doctor who could see what was happening with her.

Finally, we had a virtual visit with the primary care physician the nursing home assigned to her when she moved there four years earlier.

The "exam" took place in my mom's room with her lying back on her bed and a nursing home computer set up on a cart that had been rolled into her room minutes earlier.

The appointment was rushed because the same doctor – Dr. Donna Knupp – had other patients to see after my mother using the same computer.

With the doctor already online when the computer arrived, we got right down to business as soon as my mother settled into position.

I lifted up my mom's shirt to reveal what had grown from one red spot to multiple lesions on the left side of her chest.

I don't think any of us, including Dr. Knupp, thought this was the best way to diagnose a medical problem, but we made the best of it.

For my mom, a very modest woman, it was an intimate, somewhat awkward exam under any circumstance, but the fact that it was being done without the benefit of the doctor present in the room only added to her uneasiness.

I could see the fear and confusion on her face, and I did my best to comfort her.

It was a world of virtual medicine that my mother didn't understand. She was confused by the fact that she saw her face and the doctor's face on the computer screen at the same time.

She held my hand tightly as she looked at the screen then looked at me for guidance and clarity as if I had the secret to navigating this strange new world that she was living in.

I didn't.

Truthfully, I think all of us, the doctor included, were frustrated by our inability to be in the same room to interact and conduct a real examination.

Dr. Knupp normally was so kind and personable, putting her patients at ease with her gentle touch and a few calming words before starting an exam.

Few words were exchanged during this exam before it was decided that an ultrasound of my mother's left breast would be the next logical step.

The doctor said to sit back and wait for the test to happen. Because of the pandemic, we'd have to wait for someone to come to the nursing home to do the ultrasound.

Sit back and wait?

More time wasted, I thought.

More time lost in our battle to find what was slowly but surely taking my beautiful Evelyn away from me.

Every day, I felt like we were losing valuable time in dealing with whatever seemed to be fueling this rash and what I felt was sapping my mother's energy.

Mounting thoughts of self-doubt raced through my mind.

Should I be pushing the doctors to be more aggressive with my mother's care?

Am I asking them the right questions?

Is there something that I'm missing?

Late at night while my mother was sleeping, I'd sit in that recliner next to her and think about her situation and how I could get answers more quickly.

There has to be a better way, I thought.

In silent conversations with myself, I asked, "I'm in Pittsburgh, with some of the finest hospitals in the nation, and I can't find out what's causing this rash on my mother's chest?"

How can this be happening?

What am I doing wrong?

I never relinquished my hope that there was something – some medicine or some treatment – that would make her feel better and help her rebound.

I'd doze off to sleep every now and then, but I never really slept soundly at the nursing home.

If it wasn't my own anxiety and dark thoughts about what was happening around me, there always were voices in the hallways or the occasional cries of patients that kept me from the kind of sleep that I knew I so desperately needed.

Day after day, I was so tired.

I could see that Evelyn's health was in a rapid decline and even though I didn't want to admit it to anyone, my circumstances were beginning to take a toll on me both physically and emotionally.

One day became like the one before it and the one before that.

Get up.

Get both of us dressed.

Try to talk Evelyn into eating a little something while I'd have something from my breakfast tray.

Then there was work for me before we'd eat again and before we knew it another day had passed and it was time to get Evelyn ready for bed.

In between, there were activities, but as time passed, Evelyn's interest in those waned as her sickness drained her energy.

Everything I did was with one watchful eye on her as she slept, sometimes calling for me from her bed, sometimes stirring restlessly for no particular reason.

Watching it all fall to pieces, watching her decline so rapidly tore at my heart day after day.

One deep emotional freefall frightened me, and although I managed to pull myself out of it, it was a pivotal moment I never will forget.

Prior to logging on that day for her virtual appointment, Evelyn said she wasn't feeling well. She was especially tired and wanted to sleep, but she soldiered on, knowing we had this appointment to keep.

God love her, she always was compliant and never fought me when I told her that we needed to see a doctor for this reason or that.

Two of the nursing home workers tried to put a brace on her left hand to straighten out her fingers, which sometimes became clenched, a side effect of her stroke.

Sometimes she tolerated the brace.

This was one of those occasions when it was excruciatingly uncomfortable to wear it.

She cried out as they manipulated her hand.

Her tears and the look of absolute agony on her face was more than I could handle.

You never want to see your parents hurting and this went way beyond just a little discomfort.

I started to cry so hard that my entire body shook. I couldn't stop.

Something inside of me just exploded.

Of course, it wasn't just about the brace. It was everything around me that was out of control … spiraling … like a snowball rolling down a steep hill and there wasn't a damn thing I could do to stop it.

They gave up on the idea of the brace and apologetically left the room.

Evelyn and I both sat there sobbing,

I remember thinking that I wished I was dead.

I even wrote it in my journal that day.

Some may find my feelings extreme or even melodramatic, painting a picture of me as being emotionally unhinged.

I have to admit that today, when I look back through my journal, it is jarring to see that I wrote those words. But it's truly how I felt, not because I felt trapped and wanted to leave the nursing home, but because I thought I was failing my mother in the most epic way imaginable.

It has taken me a long time to admit this, but at that point, I remember thinking this must be how some elderly couples feel when one person is sick, and they decide that murder-suicide is the easiest way out of it all.

One can't live without the other, so neither one will live.

Thank goodness, my thoughts never sunk to that level, but it was the best analogy I could think of at the time to describe my state of mind.

It truly was one of the worst moments of my days at Charles Morris.

In my head, I knew things were headed in a bad direction and that this time we weren't going to be able to turn it around like we had so many times before.

I tried to banish any thoughts that she might not make it, but I knew that was a distinct possibility.

I also needed to prepare myself for that eventuality, but my mind wouldn't go there.

Days passed and I was able to raise myself and my emotions enough to refocus on what was happening with Evelyn's health.

I still wasn't in a great state of mind, but I was better. I had to be. I had so much to do. If I didn't advocate for Evelyn, no one else would do it.

People on the outside would continue to ask me, "Are you OK."

As my stay at Charles Morris went well past the two weeks I thought I'd be there, people would ask, "Are you going to stay?"

While I appreciated their concern, I dismissed their questions.

Was I OK? I wasn't sure, but I was getting up every day and doing what I needed to do.

Was I going to stay? There was no question, I wouldn't leave unless someone dragged me out of there.

Would I be sane at the end of it all? Well, that was another matter.

There was a day, not long after our virtual appointment when I realized that Evelyn had lost the one thing that had gotten her through the toughest days of her life – her willingness to fight.

That unshakable spirit and fortitude were gone.

And all signs indicated they weren't coming back.

Anyone who's ever been a caregiver knows that one of the earliest lessons learned is how to get someone back and forth to the bathroom.

It's a routine Evelyn and I had run through with ease on thousands of occasions.

She always wanted to do as much as possible for herself and I really was just there to steady her and make a few clothing adjustments along the way.

But this time, she wasn't able to even stand up.

She tried over and over again to boost herself to her feet, straining and struggling a little more each time.

She sunk back into her wheelchair exhausted from it all.

Despite her best efforts, her legs wouldn't support her.

She looked at me with such sadness and defeat in her eyes.

She was done.

Her fight was gone.

When she had her stroke, there had been days like this when she couldn't stand, but we fought through it with physical therapy.

She became stronger and I learned how to move her – even in my high heels – from her wheelchair to the toilet or her bed or the car with no problems.

Sure, there were tears as we, along with my dad, learned to live in Evelyn's new world that was far from their old life that was filled with bowling leagues, bocce, volunteer work and trips to Atlantic City.

But we did it.

However, now my dad was gone, and the challenges facing Evelyn and me were much more daunting.

As she sat there, unable to move, I knew this was different.

Without that strength and determination to battle whatever it was that was making her so sick, she had no chance.

I pulled the cord next to the toilet that was there to summon help if a patient or family member needed assistance.

I seldom asked for help because I felt I could handle just about anything.

But in this case, I needed it – both physically and emotionally.

A nurse and two aides came to my rescue.

After we got Evelyn situated, they hugged me.

I turned away from my mother as the tears welled up in my eyes. I didn't want her to see my crying, but the sadness just engulfed me at that moment.

I was beginning notice both physical and mental lapses with my mom.

Where was this headed? What was happening?

Evelyn settled in for an afternoon nap.

I watched her as she drifted off into a peaceful sleep.

While she slept, I sat there, intermittently staring off into space and crying over what had just happened with her.

Oh, how I loved this woman.

She had given me so much in my life and why can't I find a way to make her better?

I held Evelyn's hand.

I realized that someday that hand wouldn't be there to hold.

Someday, I would be on my own in this world without the one person who loved me without condition, who stood by me without judgment and was always there at my side when life lobbed its harshest and cruelest shots at me.

I got up, wanting to pace, but there was really nowhere to go in this tiny room that seemed to be getting smaller every day.

Within a few days, a technician arrived at the nursing home to do the ultrasound of Evelyn's left breast.

I was grateful that even though we were in lockdown, these kinds of health care workers were permitted to come into our facility to do tests such as this.

I know they were putting their lives on the line every day as the virus continued to spread – and kill – in the world outside.

A few days later, Dr. Knupp called with the results.

She was concerned about what she saw and wanted Evelyn to see a specialist at nearby UPMC Magee-Womens Hospital. Her description of the results was vague and that was worrisome.

At that stage, I already knew the news would not be good, but I went through the motions of getting ready for the next appointment, which thank goodness, would be in-person and not via computer.

I spent the afternoon of April 7 getting my mother's backpack ready to go outside.

We always took extra items when we went out. There were briefs, wipes and plastic gloves as well as a change of clothes. There also was a hat and scarf in case we needed them, and a container of thickened orange juice and sugar packets in the event her blood sugar dropped.

The next day, we were up before sunrise.

As we got ready that morning, there was little conversation.

Part of it might have been that Evelyn, who'd become accustomed to sleeping in, was still a little groggy.

We talked a little about the day, where we were going and what we would be doing.

Evelyn knew we were going out to see a doctor and I tried to explain why, but I'm not sure that she fully understood.

In reality, I had no idea what we would be doing. I certainly had no clue where any of this was headed.

She dutifully went along with what I asked her to do that morning.

She trusted me and, of course, she was happy to finally go out because it was a nice day.

Once she was up, dressed and in her wheelchair, I wheeled her into the lobby where the director of nursing made sure everyone knew they should let us back into the facility when we returned.

I felt a little like an inmate making a break for it that morning.

Perry came by at 7:15 a.m. to drive us to Magee.

Even though Perry and I hadn't hugged each other in weeks, we didn't dare touch each other for fear that he would spread germs to me from the outside world.

He greeted Evelyn and she smiled. She loved seeing him and spending time with him and it had been so long since they were together.

It was a bright, beautiful sunny spring morning. I just wish we were headed out for another reason.

I was nervous and I could tell that my mother was, too.

Maybe she did understand what I told her earlier about this appointment. Or maybe she instinctively knew that there was something really wrong with her health.

With all of us wearing masks, we carefully loaded Evelyn into the front seat. I climbed into the backseat, and we were off on the short drive to the hospital, located in a normally busy section of the city just steps from the University of Pittsburgh campus and home to UPMC's world-renowned hospitals and research facilities.

Along the way, I caught glimpses of the outside world that had changed so dramatically in the four-plus weeks I'd been in quarantine with Evelyn.

The city streets were empty as people everywhere complied with a statewide stay-at-home order.

Normally, at this hour, the streets would be springing to life with buses and cars as commuters made their way to work and school.

Not on this day.

Born and raised in the city, I'd never seen Pittsburgh look like this.

I spied a light or two on in houses along the way, but it seemed that everyone was sleeping in, waiting to return to their old lives.

At this point, covid-19 was reported in all 67 of Pennsylvania's counties.

The pandemic was worsening, and deaths were climbing.

Across the world, there were more than a million confirmed cases of the virus with the number growing every day.

People were out of work. More than 6.6 million Americans filed for their first week of unemployment benefits in the previous week, the highest number of initial claims in history.

The country was sharply divided about how the pandemic was being handled.

It was a world that I didn't recognize.

My mom clutched her rosary beads.

As we entered the lobby, I only saw a few people.

I'd been to this hospital many times to do interviews and even this early on a normal day, it would be bustling with people.

But not today.

I approached the information desk and was told I couldn't go with my mom to her appointment.

Another roadblock.

I kept my wits about me and calmly told the person at the desk that the doctor said I'd be able to accompany my mother because she was in a wheelchair.

The worker made a call and got the OK for us to move along.

With that obstacle cleared, we rode the elevator to the second floor where we sat alone in an empty waiting room.

There were signs on every other chair to keep people from sitting too close together. I sat as close to my mom as possible, never letting go of her hand.

We were called back to the exam room where I helped her remove the layers of clothes she wore that day – her black coat, a flowered jacket, a black turtleneck and her bra – and gently helped move her onto the examination table. I covered her with three blankets. Without them, I knew she'd be freezing.

Most exam tables aren't very wide and usually don't have side rails, so I kept an eye on her to make sure she didn't slip off.

The first doctor thought my mom had a skin infection, but she needed to consult a colleague.

When he looked at my mom's breast, he decided on a punch biopsy – a procedure in which a piece of skin is taken for further examination.

There were needles and blood and stitches. She went through it like a champ. It was heart-wrenching to watch, but I wanted to be there. I sat at eye level to the table and watched the entire process.

He numbed the area, then took a piece of the tissue. He stitched it so carefully. I wished it was me on that table instead of her. I didn't want her to have to go through any of this.

After the procedure, I helped her off the table into the wheelchair. I put her clothes back on. When someone can't use one of their arms, you learn to put their shirt on the weak side first and then the strong side. It's the opposite when getting them undressed.

I texted Perry that we were ready to leave.

Once again, few words were spoken on that return trip to Charles Morris.

I asked Perry to take us on a side trip.

Of course, he agreed.

All I wanted was a 30-minute ride to Juliano's, one of our favorite Italian restaurants just outside the city in Robinson Township, for some take-out food.

In reality, the fresh air that day smelled sweeter than the Italian goodies we'd pick up at Juliano's and I just didn't want that time outside to end.

When we finally landed back at Charles Morris, Evelyn was exhausted from the trip and the biopsy and just wanted to sleep.

We never spoke about the test or when the results might come in.

Maybe she didn't want to know.

Or maybe she was just too tired to care.

At that point, I think I knew the news would not be good.

Two days later, the call came from the surgeon.

He was kind, but to the point, speaking first in the medical terms that described her condition.

"Triple-negative breast cancer," he said.

"Stage 3 and aggressive," he followed.

He did not recommend surgery, chemotherapy or radiation.

As he spoke, my mind raced to think about what other options there might be to fight the cancer.

Then he delivered the final blow when he told me, "Treasure your time with her. She's lived a long life."

His words took my breath away.

I sat down, trying to steady myself.

I tried my best to maintain my composure as we talked, all the while replaying his words in my mind.

No treatment.

No surgery.

Nothing.

Treasure my time?

It was more than I could process.

After we hung up I could barely breathe, but I needed to understand what just happened.

I remembered that he mentioned palliative care, so of course I did a Google search.

One of the first entries that comes up on such a search is from Wikipedia and states, that palliative care is an "interdisciplinary medical caregiving approach aimed at optimizing quality of life and mitigating suffering among people with serious, complex and often terminal illnesses."

It said nothing about a cure or treatment.

My spirit fell about as low as I thought it could possibly go.

The day that we left the hospital, the surgeon who did the biopsy told me that my mom's rash did not look good, but he couldn't officially say anything until he received the test results.

I guess I held out some hope that his initial thoughts were wrong.

Again, I suppose I was in denial.

In hindsight, it seems that I spent a lot of time in a state of denial.

When I hung up with the surgeon, my mom was sleeping, so I had some time to collect my thoughts.

I remember looking at the Easter palms and cross on the wall and saying a little prayer, then texting my siblings.

My sister Paula got right back to me. Aside from being a nurse and the wife of a radiologist, she'd been through breast cancer herself, a double mastectomy, chemotherapy and reconstructive surgery years earlier when her now-adult children were young.

Paula knew Evelyn's situation was dire.

One by one, my siblings texted to talk about what was happening, each one taking time to digest this crushing news that was just dropped on us.

We agreed that the best we could do is keep her comfortable and free from any pain.

The next few days were a blur. I tried to remain calm in Evelyn's presence, but I'm sure she knew I wasn't myself.

Finally, I told her about the results of the biopsy. I uttered the word cancer, but I wasn't sure that in her weakened state, she fully understood.

She did say that she didn't want any treatment that would make her sick, maybe a pill now and then, but nothing else.

It was clear that she wanted no valiant efforts to prolong her life. She was ready to move on. But I wasn't.

She didn't say much more.

Maybe she needed time to digest this information.

I know that I did.

We went about our next few days together with me tiptoeing around the subject, making conversation with Evelyn about any number of mundane topics aimed at keeping my mind and hers off the elephant in the room – the cancer that seemed to be engulfing her body.

On Easter Sunday evening, Evelyn's primary care physician – Dr. Knupp – came by and called to me from my mom's doorway.

She wasn't allowed in the room because of the lockdown.

I got out of my chair and said we could meet in a nearby empty dining room.

I'd texted her the day before, but she said she didn't answer because she wanted to talk to me in person.

She was a kind woman, always trying to put my mother at ease by asking about the things she knew were important to her – church and family.

On that day, it appeared she was giving me a bit of a reality check.

She said it was time for me to think about hospice care for Evelyn.

The mere mention of the word submerged me in a flood of tears and confusion.

Suddenly, I was in a new world of terms that I'd heard, but never fully understood – palliative care and hospice care.

I came to understand on the most basic level that they are both comfort care, but that palliative care often begins at the diagnosis of a life-threatening disease, sometimes when someone is still undergoing treatment.

I also came to understand that palliative care does not mean death.

Hospice care often begins when treatment has ceased, and it is believed the patient is not going to survive.

I knew that I should consider these options and that based on my conversations with the doctors, hospice care probably was best for Evelyn.

I just had a hard time committing to it.

In my head, it all made sense. Her prognosis was poor.

But in my heart, I wasn't ready for it.

There was that battle raging between my heart and my head.

Once I signed those papers and agreed to hospice, I was accepting the fact that she was dying.

In my mind, if I didn't sign, then maybe she's not dying, I thought.

I know that sounds completely irrational, but you have to think about where I was and what I was doing.

I'm not sure about my mental state at that time. I'm not sure I would have admitted it then, but I really wasn't thinking clearly.

That same night, around 1 a.m. Evelyn woke me from a sound sleep.

She stirred for a while and then spoke just a few words that cut like a razor-sharp knife.

"I'm old. I'm not going to be around much longer," she said, before quickly going back to sleep.

It was startling and disturbing, almost as if she was trying to prepare me for what was ahead.

Sure, there were times she would say things like, "you know I'm not going to live forever."

But this was different.

When she would see people celebrating their 100th birthdays, she would say, "I don't want to live to be 100. What can you do at that age?"

But on this night, when she awoke from a sound sleep to utter these words, I'm fairly certain she was sending me a message that I just wasn't ready to hear.

We never talked about that night.

The next day, when she finally woke up about 11:30, we talked about anything except her pronouncement the night before.

I asked her about the pain she was feeling in her breast from the biopsy.

"Is your breast feeling better?"

"It's not as bad as it was," she said.

"You're tough mom," I said.

"Well, I've been through a lot of things in my life," she said.

She certainly had.

There were days when I thought we were so close to losing Evelyn, but somehow she held on.

She was given medicine every morning for her thyroid, and it had to be taken before she ate anything.

About 5:30 one morning, the night nurse came in to give her that medicine and couldn't rouse her from her sleep.

Since I was sleeping right next to her, I heard the commotion, woke up and jumped to my feet.

She took my mom's blood sugar which was 52. A normal morning reading is supposed to be in the 90-120 range.

I'd dealt with my mother's diabetes for some time and seen her blood sugar shoot up and down within a given day.

Generally, we liked to see it stay a little higher, so she didn't pass out, which wasn't a problem since Evelyn loved her sweets.

But I'd never seen her blood sugar drop to the point where she lost consciousness.

This was worse than I'd ever seen before.

I dumped two sugar packets in thickened orange juice and tried to get her to drink.

The nurse handed me a tube of sugar gel that I squeezed into her mouth.

The gel was something we used as a last resort to get her sugar level up because it sends your blood sugar skyrocketing, sometimes up to the 200-plus level.

Bleary eyed, my heart was racing as I looked for any sign that she was responding.

There was nothing.

Over and over again, I tried everything to get her to regain consciousness.

The nurse, Donna, was calm.

"We'll get her back," she said. "We'll get her."

I know it was only minutes, but it seemed like hours.

Finally, she began to come around, not knowing what had just happened.

I sat down, shaking.

Later, we talked about it, but she seemed unfazed, not remembering those frightening minutes when she slipped away from us.

I was a wreck.

Oh Evelyn, please don't do this to me again, I thought.

In the days following the low blood sugar episode, the bad news just kept on coming.

During a virtual appointment with a nephrologist – a kidney specialist – we found that my mom's kidney function was at 18%. I knew this is not good because my dad had been on kidney dialysis for 2½ years.

It was just one more strike against her.

I also knew that with all of her other health issues dialysis wasn't a possibility and that it was only a matter of time until her kidneys and other organs began to shut down.

I tried with all that I had to find ways to occupy myself to distract myself from the fact that my mother was dying right there beside me in that 250-square foot room where I lived with her night and day.

But there was no escaping it.

I talked with friends and family on the phone and by text.

I tried to work, but there were times when my mom would just cry through most of the day because of the pain and it became almost impossible for me to get anything done.

I felt helpless, not knowing how to comfort her.

"Go sit in the TV room and work and let us take care of your mother," the nursing home workers would tell me.

Once, a nursing assistant named Kandii Coleman came into the room as I was sitting there with Evelyn trying unsuccessfully to comfort her. Sensing my frustration and my sorrow, she shooed me out of the room, telling me to let her do her job while I went off to do mine.

Work provided some escape for me from all that was happening around me.

I'd sit in that big open TV room by myself with just my phone and my laptop writing stories about how the rest of the world was working its way through the pandemic and how life might never be the same for any of us.

Every once in a while, my mind would wander to my co-workers out there covering this once-in-a-lifetime story of the illness that shut down the world.

I'd think about their feelings of exhilaration as journalists to be providing such important information to our readers, but also their fear that came with being out there in public where the virus was still spreading unchecked.

Every once in a while, I'd hear about someone from the office who contracted the virus, though, thank God, they all recovered.

Day after day, I sat there making calls for my stories about groups trying to raise funds when in-person fundraisers were no longer possible, about kids who were trying to learn when they were no longer permitted in their classrooms and businesses struggling to survive by getting goods and services to their customers in any way they could.

Every once in a while, a care package would be delivered to the nursing home for us from a friend or a family member.

Sometimes it was the simplest gestures that touched me.

Rosie's daughter-in-law brought me a new polka dot mask, which was beautiful.

My sister Rose sent an old-fashioned bingo machine for Evelyn. Rose always sends the best gifts.

I hoped and prayed there was time left to use it.

More often that support came from Perry.

Perry never failed us. He also never questioned what I was doing or why I was doing it. He was behind me every step of the way.

Two years later, Perry still says he knew it was what had to happen and has never second-guessed my decision to quarantine with my mother.

Sure, he worried about me, he said, but he knew I was exactly where I needed to be.

There really was no other option, he said.

By May 1 – Day 50, my mom's nurse told me to let Evelyn eat whatever she wants because her weight had plummeted from a high of 140 pounds to about 90 pounds.

That night, she had wedding soup and carrot cake. She ate slowly, as if it was a chore and without the gusto she once had for two of her favorite foods.

After dinner, we had a visit from Rabbi Eli Seidman who would stop in most Saturdays to check on us.

Evelyn and I both found his voice and his presence so calming and would watch his weekly service on TV, even though we weren't familiar with all the traditions and meanings of the Jewish service.

But despite our different religions, he saw the importance of our faith and spirituality to us and made sure a priest was there for us when we needed him.

He was a gift to us in so many ways.

Later that night, as I pushed my mom around the unit in her wheelchair, we stopped near one of the windows.

Even though she spent most days sleeping, I still tried to get her up in her wheelchair when I could, even if was only for a short time.

By now, she looked so tired and so beaten down, but she mustered the strength to look up at me and say, "It looks so nice out there."

I told her I agreed.

I knew she wanted to go out.

When you can't go out, you look at the outdoors differently. You notice the sun and the blue sky. You crave air blowing on your face.

I wanted so badly to rip open that door and take my mom outside and let her feel that sunshine and breathe that air, just one more time.

I wanted to forget the rules, but I knew I couldn't.

It was such a simple request and I felt so awful that I kept turning her down.

On May 11, I looked at the calendar and realized we'd made it to Day 60.

It was two months – far from the 14 days we thought this lockdown would last when we started it back in March.

I thought about all that had happened in those months.

I was tired but didn't want to admit it. I was scared but didn't want to mouth those words.

I knew that in four days, we had an in-person appointment with Evelyn's oncologist at UPMC Magee and I expected that there would be some more difficult news delivered during that appointment.

By this time, the lesions on my mother's chest were oozing and bleeding and the pain from the biopsy was, at times, unbearable.

The doctor said that if the bleeding continued, we could consider radiation treatments.

I didn't respond, knowing that I didn't want to subject my mother to anything that would cause her additional discomfort.

Again, the subject of palliative care came up.

I listened but didn't commit to anything. I still wasn't ready to sign those papers.

Even though the news was not good, I felt a calmness in her office. She took her time and talked with us, commenting that she wasn't aware that I'd been living in lockdown with my mother.

We talked about my mom being in pain from the punch biopsy. These biopsies can take weeks to heal, she told us.

Finally, there was the gut punch.

She said it was likely that Evelyn had months, not years left.

Months?

It was the first time someone had assigned a timeline to it all.

An endpoint.

It wasn't what I wanted to hear.

I wasn't ready for this news.

No one ever is.

Surely, on some level, I knew that her life was ending, but again, denial is a strong emotion and I know now that I was not in the best state of mind at the time.

Was I hoping for some miracle cure? Maybe.

Was I thinking that my 93-year-old mother would live forever? Perhaps.

My thinking and my view of the world was so clouded at this stage that I'm just not sure what I was thinking or why.

I knew that I needed to let my brother and sisters know this latest news right away.

I wanted to give them the chance to come and say goodbye.

Because there are so many of us, I'd communicated with my siblings mostly through texts. With all of us in different states, it seemed easiest.

I'd do group texts before and after appointments.

Looking back, I think I did it by text because I didn't want to talk in front of my mother, and I didn't want to get too far away from her.

It also spared me the pain of retelling the same story four times.

But it was important to keep them in the loop about Evelyn's illness. I had her medical power of attorney, but I would have never made these decisions without them.

We're a unit, we do these kinds of things together.

We learned that kind of teamwork from our parents.

At some point, it made sense to not sleep on my cot anymore and just place the recliner close to Evelyn's bed because she'd been waking up so often through the night.

To be honest, at that point, I wasn't sleeping much anyway, so the chair was fine for me to catch a quick nap now and then.

I was there when she reached for me or cried out in her sleep.

I'd try my best to reassure her, holding her hand and usually getting her back to sleep for a short time before the next stab of pain or bad dream woke her.

When morning came, I tried to stick with our routine as much as possible, but that became more challenging as time passed.

Evelyn always wore her dentures and put them in first thing in the morning.

But lately, she'd been having trouble getting them to stay in place because she'd lost so much weight.

All her life, my mother struggled with tooth and gum issues. She wore partials and dentures for most of her life. Just another curse that had been dealt to her, but she handled it and never complained.

Without her dentures, eating became more difficult, so we switched gears to give her mostly soup and ice cream, just to get some nourishment into her.

When people on the outside heard about this, the deliveries of soup and Evelyn's favorite strawberry ice cream began pouring in without fail.

Honestly, I wouldn't have survived without outside help from my husband, and friends who treated us to pizzas, lots of pasta and wedding soup from Big Jim's, as well as home-cooked meals.

Of course, we enjoyed the food, but it was the love and caring that food represented that buoyed us.

It made us feel like we weren't alone and we weren't forgotten.

One night, as I was about to fall asleep, Evelyn reached for me and patted me on the head.

She didn't say anything.

I looked at my phone. It was 2 a.m.

I would often reach for her too throughout the night, because when you are scared, no matter how old you are, you still want your mother.

And these days, I was scared.

I'm not sure what was different about this particular night, but the next morning I scheduled an appointment with a member of the hospice and palliative care team.

I knew it was time.

During my appointment, we talked about hospice and how my mom would get attention from nurses and aides right there in the same room where we had been living for months. There would be support for me, too.

It was a lot to process.

Hospice is a tough word to hear when it is in regard to someone you love.

The word attaches a sense of urgency about the here and now because you don't know if there is a tomorrow.

We discussed medications to keep my mom pain-free and how they'd begin to cut out some of her other medications.

I still struggled with accepting the notion of hospice, but I knew that I didn't want my mother to suffer.

"There is no crystal ball to tell us how long she has left," the hospice worker told me.

We talked for a while in my mom's room and then we went to the television room to sign the papers.

I cried as I signed my name.

There is absolutely nothing that prepares you for this moment, even though, in your head, you know it's coming.

I sat there for a while, thinking about what I'd done. In my entire life, I'd never done anything as important.

Finally, I realized I needed to dry my tears and pull myself together.

I needed some "Rosie time."

Without fail, Rosie always made me feel better.

When I stopped by her room, of course, she wanted to play cards.

Although I knew there was no chance on God's green earth that I could ever beat her, I needed her gentle demeanor and calming wisdom more than she could ever imagine at that moment.

Sitting there with her on her bed, I looked at her and thanked the good Lord for giving her to me.

I won two games, but she won three.

She said, "good thing we aren't playing for money."

I agreed with a chuckle.

Oh Rosie, if you only knew how much I love you, I thought.

My mom had a bad night from the pain of the biopsy.

She kept saying "I'm sick, I'm sick."

In the middle of the night, she woke up and we talked about cancer and what that meant.

It was the first time we'd talked in any great detail about her diagnosis.

She told me again that she didn't want any drastic measures. I held her hand. We cried. We both knew that cancer was winning this battle and there wasn't anything we could do.

There was a sense that time was winding down.

Finally, she drifted off and the conversation stopped.

I watched my mom as she slept.

I didn't know what would happen in the coming days, but I knew one thing. I would be right there by her side every step of the way.

I'm here for you Evelyn, I thought to myself. I will not leave your side for anything or anybody.

Chapter 7 –

About Me

THE TIME THAT I SPENT at Charles Morris was supposed to be about my mother, not me ... just my mother, pure and simple.

But there were days when the emotions bubbled up inside of me and it became about me and how I was handling the strain of being there and the unimaginable thoughts of losing my mother.

I'd look at her lying in bed and want to tell her how much I loved her and beg her not to leave me.

We needed more time together.

There were more talks for us to have, more places for us to go.

I realized that she was 93 and she'd had a full life.

But I selfishly wanted more.

I realize now that some of my thoughts of wanting so desperately to hold onto her probably sound irrational.

But rational thoughts were in short supply some days as cancer tightened its grip on my mother.

Some people also would find it strange that not only did I want more time with Evelyn, but I also wanted more time with the people with whom I'd become close to at Charles Morris.

The workers and the residents there had become my family through the most difficult days of my life, and I didn't want to leave them.

I knew that once Evelyn was gone, my relationship with them would never be the same. The intimacy of that relationship would be gone. Our common bond – taking care of Evelyn – would cease to exist and I would be an outsider looking into their world.

I didn't want to lose Evelyn and them. But I knew it was a very real possibility.

Day in and day out, my world was one giant ball of angst.

Some days, I wondered what had happened to my old life, that life that had gone on without me since I walked through the doors of this nursing home on March 13?

Then there was my home, my husband, my friends, all on the outside, all going on with their lives, while my world was limited to these four walls.

I wondered what had changed and how different it would all look to me after my experience.

By the beginning of May, Gov. Wolf slowly began lifting the stay-at-home order for Pittsburgh and many of the surrounding counties, permitting retailers and other businesses to reopen.

After months of working remotely, plans were underway at my company for everyone to gradually return to work at the end of May and beginning of June.

Perry had gone on for months now without me at home, although to be honest, for the last 16 ½ years, while I was taking care of my parents, he was so often on his own.

Through it all, he never questioned my devotion to my parents, never resented the time that I spent with them, even when I decided to quarantine with Evelyn. He was supportive and on my worst days at Charles Morris, he was there for me.

Maybe it was only by phone or by text, but he was there.

He always has been.

On May 5, Evelyn and I were up most of the night.

She was restless and in constant pain.

The best I could offer was a hand to hold and a few occasional words of comfort. It all seemed so inadequate.

In the darkness of the room, I tried to hide my tears from my mom. I'm not sure how successful I was, but I did my best.

The problem was that I spent so much time crying that I'm pretty sure she saw me but was too weak to say anything.

I'd sent a text to the director of nursing, Kris Cyr, around 4 a.m. and she said she'd stop by before she started her shift.

At 5 a.m. she knocked on the door.

I was slouched in the blue recliner, wearing the same clothes I'd worn the day before, covered with a white comforter.

I'd gotten to the point where I didn't care what I was wearing or what I looked like, which on the outside world, was totally out of character for me.

But day-old clothes were the least of my worries.

I pulled on my hat and quietly told her to, "come in."

I tried to wipe away my tears, but I'm sure she could tell I was crying by the deep, dark eyeliner and mascara smudges under my eyes.

Looking fresh and rested in her white lab coat, she sat across from me on my cot.

In the time my mom had been at the nursing home Kris was always calm, always in control, even when things appeared to be going sideways.

She'd always been a source of comfort for me.

"You are a wonderful daughter," she began.

I was shuddering at the thought of what she was about to say.

I knew what was coming next – things were not well with my mom, but my heart just wasn't ready to hear it. It never would be ready.

She said: "JoAnne should think about what JoAnne will do next."

I know I looked at her with a puzzled expression.

The thought had not even crossed my mind.

For the past 16 ½ years, my mom and dad were my everything.

Every day revolved around them and their needs.

I know that in the process, I probably neglected other parts of my life, including Perry.

We sat and talked for a while, but I'm not sure that I remember all of the conversation.

Those few words echoed in my head.

I couldn't think about what I would do next.

I wasn't ready to think about JoAnne, as Kris had suggested.

I wasn't ready for that chapter of my life. I didn't want to turn the page to the next chapter without Evelyn.

After Kris left, I cried for what seemed like an eternity until exhaustion apparently took over and I fell asleep, all twisted up in my chair, still wearing those same rumpled clothes.

When I woke up, I looked around the room, remembering my talk with Kris.

I knew she was right.

But I couldn't think about it.

I wouldn't think about it.

As my mom's condition worsened, I was feeling more frazzled, and the simplest turn of events touched off waves of spontaneous tears that proved increasingly difficult to quell.

It also became increasingly difficult to hide them from my mother.

Sometimes she'd ask me what was wrong and why I seemed so sad.

Most days, I'd offer some vague answer, hoping she'd buy my flimsy explanation.

"Oh, it's just everything, Mom. It's that rash on your chest and we can't go outside," I'd tell her.

Sometimes I'd tell her that I was worried about work.

"I'm just worried about doing my job while I'm in here," I'd say.

I'm not sure that she ever really believed me.

After dinner one night, I said, I decided to see if I could get her out of bed and into her wheelchair for a trip down the hall to look out her favorite window.

I probably did it as much for me as I did it for her.

Carol Danhires photo

As Evelyn becomes weaker, JoAnne takes advantage of a warm day to grant her mother's wish to go outside.

Once at the window, I looked at her and wondered when that day would come when I could no longer wheel her to this "window on her world" that she loved so much.

The sadness I felt was overwhelming.

She had a stark, pale pallor and was getting weaker by the day, but she mustered the energy to slowly make her standard request that, as usual, broke my already fragile heart:

"It looks so nice out there. Can we go out?"

"No, mom, I'm so sorry, we can't," my voice cracking as I answered her.

"This virus is pretty bad, isn't it," she said, obviously forgetting that she had mouthed the same words just hours earlier.

I didn't answer.

I couldn't.

With tears in my eyes, I grabbed the handles of the wheelchair and pushed her back to our room where I sat down with her.

There was so much I wanted to say, but I was at a loss for words.

I just sat there with her for a moment, looking at her and trying to capture this snapshot of her in my mind.

I didn't want to ever forget what she looked like or sounded like. I wanted to sear the memories of my time with Evelyn in my mind, so that one day, when she was gone, I could reach back and replay them.

I'm not sure that she fully understood the toll that all of this was taking on me, how tired I felt, how often I cried or the sheer panic I felt when the situation was so out of control.

But again, it really wasn't about me.

It was about her.

I wasn't the one dying, but there were days when I felt that little by little, I WAS dying, that this lockdown was sucking the life out of me.

I didn't dare admit any of this to anyone back then. I would have been too guilt-ridden to do that. I needed to be strong. And for some time afterwards, I never admitted how much of me I lost during my time at Charles Morris.

I was a happy person, but that joy was gone. I was strong, but that strength was waning with each passing day.

Inwardly, in conversations with myself, I wondered if I would ever be the same and if I could ever be happy again.

I'd sunk so low, I didn't know if I could ever climb back out to where I was before March 13 and I began this lockdown.

By early May, deep, crippling anxiety became a constant in my world.

And even the simplest routine events, such as a fire drill, could catapult me into full-blown panic.

Early one morning, my sleep was broken by the wail of the fire alarm.

I jumped straight up, not knowing what was happening, not knowing if there was a fire or if it was a drill.

If it was a test, I knew what to do – close the door to our room and wait for someone to let us know everything was OK.

On this day, it was just that.

I tried to fall back to sleep, but my mind was running wild with worry.

I started to think about what I would have done if there had been a real fire.

Lying on my cot, staring at the ceiling, I ran through the details.

We were on the second floor.

How would I get my mother out safely since we would not be able to use the elevators?

I'd have to carry her, I thought.

How would I help Rosie get out?

My fears were not without merit.

I tried to put those thoughts out of my mind, but I couldn't.

I looked over at Evelyn. She was sleeping soundly, holding on to the pink stuffed animal she bought at the gift shop.

If I had to carry her out of a burning building, I would have.

I would have found a way to get her and Rosie out of there.

I would have, I know I would.

I cried at the thought of how that scenario might have played out.

My heart raced. The fear was overwhelming.

That night, I was glad when one of the 3-to-11 p.m. workers said they were ordering dinner from LongHorn Steakhouse. I jumped at the chance. Steak sounded so much better than the peanut butter and jelly sandwich I planned to eat.

In my very small and limited world at Charles Morris, food was important. Meals became the highlight of my day and when there was a chance to eat something a little out of the ordinary, I jumped at it.

After dinner, we watched the Pirates' John Candelaria's no-hitter from Aug. 9, 1976, on AT&T SportsNet. The station was showing a lot of old games since there still was no live baseball.

Evelyn dozed on and off through the game, but I think she enjoyed it.

Those old games offered some escape from reality for us, evoking memories of happier days gathered around the TV with my mom and dad watching the Pirates back in their heyday. Those were happy times for all of us, sitting around yelling at the TV, questioning the umpires' calls and celebrating the Bucs' wins.

Simple pleasures, but oh so sweet.

If only for a couple of hours, those old games made me smile.

But on that night, not long after I turned off the TV, there was a knock at the door that brought me back to reality in an instant.

An administrator stopped by to tell me one of the employees on another wing tested positive for covid-19.

While covid cut a deadly swath through the rest of the world, we had managed to escape it at Charles Morris.

I froze. I didn't react. I didn't ask any questions. I just listened.

The worker was sent home as were other workers on that side of the hall, the administrator said.

All residents were going to be tested.

This virus now became real.

Until now, it had been distant.

Now it was just down the hall.

I worried about what came next.

Weeks before that Charles Morris employee tested positive for covid-19, the governor laid out a color-coded, three-phase plan that would permit the state to slowly – and I stress the word slowly – reopen.

I caught glimpses of the news now and then and wondered what all this might mean to me and my quarantine with Evelyn.

Would Charles Morris reopen to visitors?

Would I be able to leave?

Did I even want to leave?

I knew that plans were underway at my office to have the staff return at some point in the near future.

But I also knew that tensions were running high in the state and nation.

People were fearful about the reopening. Some dismissed the idea of a vaccine, claiming it was ineffective, dangerous, even sinister.

Businesses were struggling.

Health department officials everywhere were under fire for their handling of the pandemic.

I also heard that one county over from where I was staying, there was a nursing home where hundreds were sickened by the virus and dozens were dead.

I was grateful to be in my protective shell far from where all of the discord was occurring.

So far, all had gone well at Charles Morris.

I had faith that it would continue that way.

Much earlier, employees received new tan uniforms that they changed into each day when they arrived at the facility and changed out of before going home.

They wore protective gear everywhere and were super-mindful of ensuring that residents maintained safe distances from each other.

Safety was at the top of everyone's list.

I prayed often and earnestly.

By the end of my stay there, only one employee and no patients contracted the virus.

My prayers were answered.

By mid May, the patients and families were weary and desperately missing their loved ones after two months of being separated.

For many of these elderly people, it was the longest they'd ever been apart from their families, and it was beginning to take a toll.

Though they understood the quarantine was in place to protect them, some of them had lapsed into deep states of sadness and depression. It wasn't fair that this is how they would be spending the last days of their lives.

Administrators announced that for Mother's Day, an area in the gift shop would be set up where families could sit outside and visit with patients through a window in the side of the building.

It wasn't ideal, but under the circumstances, it was enough to lift the spirits of these poor souls who longed to see their kids and grandkids after so much time apart.

My brother Dave planned to drive in from Ohio for an in-person visit with my mom along with Perry.

Dave also would take part in a virtual visit on my computer with Evelyn and my other three siblings that morning.

Mother's Day always had been a special day for our family, and we planned to do everything we could to make this one – likely our last Mother's Day with Evelyn – as memorable as it could be under the circumstances.

There was so much to celebrate about Evelyn.

And heaven knows, she loved a good celebration of any kind.

Birthdays, holidays, anniversaries, you name it, and Evelyn would be there to mark the occasion.

She took great care in making beautiful birthday cakes for each of us. Whatever we wanted, she'd make it for us, and it would be absolutely delicious.

Of course, mine always was chocolate cake with chocolate icing.

Although there were five kids, she always made each one of us feel special on our birthdays and on holidays. I don't know where she found the time and energy, but she did, and we all remember it.

Thanksgiving and Christmas were big Italian meals, the kind that you stuff yourself with then fall asleep around the TV afterwards.

In that respect, I guess I'm a lot like her. I love a good party … and a good Italian meal.

I don't cook as much as she did. She cooked every single day. Whatever was on sale at the market, we ate all week. If it was ground meat, it was spaghetti and meatballs one day, meatloaf the next, hamburgers the next and so on.

I do know how to make her spaghetti, chocolate chip cookies and nut rolls.

A few days before Mother's Day, the nursing home's hair stylist came to our room to do Evelyn's hair and although she was so weak, I did see a glint of a smile on her face as the stylist finished.

She always loved to get her hair done, maybe once a month. If it was her birthday or Mother's Day, we'd head to her favorite Greenfield salon – Salon Louie – for a little pampering.

It wasn't something that she had the luxury of doing when she was raising five kids, but I made sure that she got there once I was an adult.

When we signed on to my computer for the virtual visit that morning, everyone gushed over how great she looked.

In reality, I know everyone was all too aware of how tired and frail she looked that day.

Though still somewhat confused about how she could see everyone's faces on the screen at the same time, she seemed pleased that all of her kids were together, even if it was via computer.

Just like old times, the conversation flowed smoothly and freely with everyone talking about what was happening in their lives.

I talked about the stories I was working on for the newspaper.

My sisters Ruth and Paula talked about the gifts they received for Mother's Day.

Dave told her he'd see her a little later that day after he drove to Pittsburgh after celebrating Mother's Day with his wife and kids.

Rose talked about what was happening with her life in New York City.

Evelyn grinned as everyone talked.

The most precious gifts this life had given her – her five kids – were all there in front of her.

Right after that virtual visit, as promised, Dave, jumped in his car and made the 2 ½ hour drive from his house in Mentor, Ohio to Pittsburgh for the window visit with Evelyn.

By necessity, window chats were limited to 15 minutes so all of the patients' families had time to meet.

But those 15 minutes were so worth it, everyone agreed.

Later that day, once Dave and Perry were in place outside the window and Evelyn and I were on other side of the glass, Dave dialed my cell phone and I put him on my speaker.

I initially felt sorry for Dave because he had to drive so far for a 15-minute visit, but I think he was happy to get out on the road that day, given the fact that everyone was still locked up in their houses because of the pandemic.

In so many ways, after my dad's death, Dave assumed the role of the "man of the family," taking care of the types of things that my dad would have handled, and always making sure that he was there for my mom and his sisters.

He always had such a gentle way with her ... and he never failed her or us.

On this day, my mom was confused by the window visit and why Dave and Perry were sitting outside, and we were on the other side of the glass window.

Marcellina Hoskowicz photo
Evelyn's son-in-law, Perry and son, Dave pay her and JoAnne a 'window visit' on Mother's Day.

"Can't they come in," she kept asking, pointing to the window.

"No mom, they can't. We have to stay here inside, and they have to be outside, but isn't it great to see them both?" I asked her.

Once again, I had to deny her this simple request and tried to steer the conversation to other matters, talking about Dave's trip there and how Perry was managing to teach his kids while the schools were still closed for in-person learning.

When it was time for Dave and Perry to leave, there was a sadness that overcame all of us. We didn't want to leave. We didn't want to say goodbye.

Still confused by the entire situation, Evelyn raised her hand to say goodbye. We all talked about "seeing you again soon." We hoped that would happen.

I prayed there was time for more visits, even if they were through the protective glass of a gift shop window.

That night, Perry brought us our Mother's Day dinner from Big Jim's, his attempt at bringing a little normalcy to a day that was anything but normal.

Most Mother's Days, we'd end up at Big Jim's then maybe at the casino or a baseball game with Evelyn as the guest of honor.

By the end of this Mother's Day, Evelyn was bone tired without ever leaving Charles Morris.

I'd hoped she enjoyed her day and all the attention she received. I wanted her to feel special, to feel loved.

That night, as I got my mom ready for bed, I told her I loved her and she said, "I love you JoAnne."

And then I asked our longtime traditional follow-up question that dated back to when I was a little girl: "All the time or most of the time?"

Usually, when I had asked that question, she would say "most of the time," because "no one loves another person all of the time."

But tonight, she looked over at me at said, "All of the time."

"Me too, Evelyn. Me too. I love you all of the time," I told her.

Chapter 8 –

The Long Goodbye

ONE AFTERNOON IN LATE MAY, Evelyn woke up and seemed to have a sudden urge to talk after days of little interaction with me or anyone else.

I jumped to my feet and went to her side, asking if she was OK.

She was groggy and spoke about all her favorite topics – the weather and how I was doing.

It also seemed that she wanted to get out of bed and into her wheelchair.

The weather outside was clear and warm, so I decided that I'd take her to the first-floor patio, an outdoor spot where we could get some fresh air and still comply with the rules of the quarantine.

It always had been one of our favorite places.

Once there, we didn't say much. We just sat next to each other, holding hands and watching the few cars traveling back and forth on Browns Hill Road.

The warmth of the sun and the gentle breeze felt so good.

The seasons were about to change and I realized this might be the last time that Evelyn would experience this special time of the year when everything around us springs to life, when the dull brown hues of winter begin to turn to green and the temperatures turn warmer with each day.

Thinking about that made the day even more beautiful to me.

Evelyn seemed to take a moment to soak it all in and then, for the second time in recent weeks, she suddenly turned to me and said, "I'm old. I'm not going to be around much longer."

I didn't respond.

I just held her hand a little more tightly and realized that this time, she was right.

At that moment, I was so grateful to be there with her.

Maybe this is why all of the pieces came together in March to let me do this, I thought.

Maybe fate intervened so that she wouldn't be alone at the end of her life.

Maybe this was God's plan, his way of ensuring that Evelyn felt safe and loved in the same way she'd made everyone in her life feel for so many years.

Suddenly, the months in quarantine, the sacrifices and the pain for me seemed all worth it. I couldn't have imagined not doing it and not being with her.

I looked at her, now so tiny and frail in that big wheelchair, and squeezed her hand realizing that she wasn't fighting what was ahead for her. There was a peacefulness about her that day.

So why couldn't I achieve that same acceptance?

Not long after, she had an exceptionally restless night when she became extremely agitated and kept moving her right arm up and down, occasionally pressing it against her face.

I watched her, trying to hold her hand, trying to reassure her that I was there, and everything was OK, but nothing seemed to work.

I didn't know if she was dreaming or if she was trying to tell me something.

"Mom, I'm here," I told her.

The hospice nurse came in, gave her some medication and asked me to step into the hallway to talk.

She said Evelyn's behavior signaled that the end of her life was near.

I took a deep breath, steadying myself against the wall and listened.

Though they were words I didn't want to hear, I knew she was right.

These hospice nurses will tell you that there are textbook signs that a person is beginning to shut down, that the body is beginning to prepare itself for death.

They've seen it so often that they know the signs as they begin to appear, and they try to prepare the families for what's ahead.

Although I'd known for weeks that this was coming, it was surreal to hear the nurse speak those words about Evelyn.

The "end of her life?"

It couldn't be.

Through my tears, I took another deep breath and texted everyone in the family to let them know what was happening.

The hospice nurse stressed that if my siblings wanted to see our mother one last time, they should come sooner rather than later.

Because of the circumstances, the nursing home would permit immediate family to enter the facility to say their goodbyes.

But they needed to come now.

On May 30 – our 79th day in quarantine – my brother, Dave, arrived from Ohio.

The three of us had some wine from a bottle that Rosie's granddaughter Jessie dropped off for us along with some food.

I left the room for half an hour or so they could have some time together. I knew this undoubtedly would be the last time he'd have the chance to talk with her.

As the only boy, my mom and my brother always were especially close. He'd been so protective of her and became even more so after my dad died.

My sisters and I always joked about him being the favorite, but we knew that Evelyn loved all of her kids equally.

Later, Dave told me that en route to Pittsburgh that day, he couldn't help but replay some of his best moments with our parents.

Like me, he wanted more time with Evelyn, but he had to accept God's will and focused on the fact that he would be able to have this one last visit with her.

He said the staff at Charles Morris couldn't have been any kinder as they outfitted him with a gown, mask and other protective gear before making the trip through the building to our mom's room.

He said Evelyn lapsed in and out of consciousness during his visit, though he was told that even people in comas can hear what's being said to them, so he was hopeful she realized he was there.

Dave later recounted his touching conversation for me.

He said that after I left the room, he told Evelyn how lucky he was that she was his mother.

"I thanked her for all the things she'd done for me over my entire life, basically helping me to grow up to become the person that I am today. I told her that I appreciated all of the good conversations we had and the good advice that she gave me over the years," he said, remembering that conversation.

He sat quietly with her for a few minutes just watching her sleep until he was told that since the nursing home was limiting the length of visits, it was time for him to think about leaving.

Later, Perry came to say his goodbyes.

He too, sat quietly with her, speaking in soft tones and thanking her for being such a great mother-in-law, thanking her for loving him.

Neither Dave nor Perry are criers. I guess I have the market cornered on that in the family, but I know these last visits were difficult for both of them.

When they left Evelyn's room after their visits, they were both clearly shaken. I knew they both were losing someone who had been such a big part of their lives.

I also know them both so well and have never seen such deep sorrow in their eyes as I saw on that day.

Evelyn and Perry had made so many memories together.

My mom always has treated him like a son, not a son-in-law. She'd always been so proud of him.

She was sleepy during his visit, but I'm sure she knew he was there.

I wondered what she was thinking when she saw Dave and Perry at her bedside or even if she was aware of the parade of final goodbyes that was playing out that week in her room.

The next day, one of the hospice workers came by and sang "Amazing Grace," to me and my mother, who continued to drift in and out of consciousness all day.

The singer had a beautiful voice and although the song always has been so meaningful to me, it's now taken on an all-new significance.

I sobbed as he sang the profoundly moving and spiritual verses that offer a message of salvation and peace:

"Amazing grace
How sweet the sound
That saved a wretch like me.
I once was lost, but now I'm found.
Was blind, but now I see.

'Twas grace that taught my heart to fear.
And grace my fears relieved.
How precious did that grace appear.
The hour I first believed.

The Lord hath promised good to me,
His word my hope secures;
He will my shield and portion be,
As long as life endures

When we've been there ten thousand years,
Bright shining as the sun,
We've no less days to sing God's praise.
Than when we first begun"

Such a soulful song.

And now, it always will make me think of that moment when I realized the wisdom of those verses and the comfort that my mother's faith always has brought to her.

I am thankful that her suffering will be over, but I fear what's ahead for me. In the coming days, I will lean on my faith to get through it all.

Days later, my mom's wheelchair sat empty.

The wheelchair that had logged what seemed like thousands of miles over 16 ½ years sat motionless in the corner while she received her first dose of morphine from the hospice nurse.

Morphine can serve many purposes. It can relieve pain, but it also can ease the breathing problems and the anxiety of trying to catch one's breath that many hospice patients experience, I learned.

The date was June 1, 2020 – our 81st day in quarantine – and for the first time, Evelyn wasn't strong enough to get out of bed.

What I would have given to hear her comment about what a beautiful day it was and ask me if we could go outside.

But not today.

Today she slept.

The rash on her chest was inflamed.

It was bleeding.

Every now and then, she would wince in pain, then begin to cry.

She'd become pitifully thin.

I'd tuck the pink stuffed pig that she loved so much under her right arm and cover her with her favorite blankets when the chills would come, especially on the left side of her body where most of the cancerous lesions had formed.

Each blanket meant something to her – the leopard print from my sister-in-law Cindi, the gray one that Rosie's son and daughter-in-law bought her as a birthday present and that pink one with white pom poms, a gift from Carol, the daughter of her friend Matilda.

When I'd looked at the calendar earlier, I remembered that June 1, 2015, was the day I took my dad to UPMC-Shadyside Hospital for the last time.

There were too many similarities to my dad's last days and that frightened me.

His death was painful for all of us to watch as my brother, Perry, my mom and I stood vigil, watching the life slowly drain from his body.

I'd taken him to the hospital from Schenley Gardens, not knowing it would be the beginning of the end for him.

Two years of kidney dialysis had been hard on him, but he was a trouper.

On that day, he was having a hard time breathing.

Once at the hospital, doctors whisked him away from me because his lung had collapsed.

They moved him to intensive care where I stayed with him, sleeping in a wooden chair all night until a dialysis machine arrived the next morning, but by then, he'd grown so much weaker.

He had no appetite.

His cardiologist – Dr. Olga Shabalov – stopped by and tried to feed him some yogurt, but he couldn't swallow it.

She looked at me and told me there was nothing more that could be done for him.

Cherish the time I had left with him, she said.

Those had become all-to-familiar words.

That day, Evelyn sat in her wheelchair at his bedside and cried.

He was breathing with the help of a machine and was conscious off and on through the day.

He tried, with every ounce of strength, to stay with her, doing dialysis three times a week for two years.

He died at 11:50 p.m. on June 6.

But now his fight was over.

As an unwilling veteran of watching someone die, I knew the end was near for Evelyn.

I wanted her pain to end, but in much the same way that she didn't want my dad to leave her, I wasn't ready for her to leave me.

I knew I couldn't have it both ways.

I felt my dad's presence on this day in a way I had not felt it before.

Maybe he was there in the room, waiting for her, waiting to take her with him so they could be together again.

On June 2, my mom slept most of the day. She had a temperature of 100.3 and was given liquid Tylenol. The nurse put her on 2 liters of oxygen.

I'm not sure why I recorded all of these details. I knew how this story was going to end, regardless of the treatment she was given.

I sat there for hours on end listening to the constant humming of the equipment aimed at making my mom's last days more tolerable.

I'd get up and pace around the room, not wanting to leave her side.

I'd stop and look at her when I thought the time between breaths seemed too long.

I'd hold my breath until she took another breath.

I squirmed in every way imaginable to try to get comfortable in that old blue recliner next to her bed, while I stared at her sleeping, thinking how it was going to feel when she took that last breath and was gone from my life forever.

The staff came by to check on us more often than usual, bringing me snacks and hugs, even though hugs were not encouraged during the pandemic.

As you sit facing the end of someone's life, you think about what really does matter.

I thought about how grateful I was to be born to these parents and how grateful I was for all that they sacrificed for me.

I wished they didn't have to struggle so much in their lives and work so hard. I wished that Paul had more time for golf and she had more bingo games. I wished that they both didn't have to worry about every nickel and dime and how they were going to keep us all fed and clothed for so many years.

But in the end, I think they were happy, and I think they were proud of what they accomplished in their lifetimes.

Although it may sound trite and I can't remember who said it first, death really is that great equalizer.

Death is death and it doesn't matter how rich or poor, how well-educated or how many material things a person has, death looks and feels the same. It has the same finality regardless of whether you drive a Porsche or a Ford.

I think that although my mom didn't have much money at the end of her life, she had a rich life. I can only hope for the same at the end of my life.

I thought about how the simplest things gave her the greatest joy.

A dice bracelet that Carol, the Charles Morris activities director gave her, was her favorite accessory because of her love for the casino.

A simple hat and scarf in the winter was all she needed to complete her outfit and she loved the off-white fleece coat that Colleen, one of the nursing assistants, gave her.

Photos of the family that she and my dad built together were her most prized possessions.

It wasn't money or purses or material things that mattered. It was the memories.

Looking around her room, I realized that it was jammed with so much – including those photos – but I refused to pack up anything because I never wanted to give up hope.

I clutched my mom's rosary beads, and I prayed. I learned that from her. Religion was important. I thought of all those Sundays she dressed the five of us for church – no jeans or tennis shoes or T-shirts.

Our Catholic upbringing gave each of us a solid foundation.

When asked questions to complete her living will, she requested a funeral Mass.

She believes in heaven and so do I.

I was just hoping to delay her trip to eternity. But that's not for me to decide.

In these final days I wanted to stay close, not knowing when she might slip away.

I tried to write some stories, but I have to admit it was tough.

I would hold my mom's hand with my left hand and try to type with my right. I wanted her to know that I was there and that she was not alone.

I would talk to her about the story I was writing.

Sometimes, I'd talk about a memory I had from my childhood.

Often, I told her how much I loved her.

Although she seldom responded, the hospice workers assured me she could hear me. I hope they were right.

I wanted her to know I kept my promise to dad to be with her no matter what.

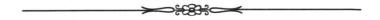

My sister, Ruth, came from New Jersey to visit on June 3. My brother-in-law Gregg drove her to Pittsburgh and waited in the car.

She told me recently that to this day, the face mask the nursing home provided to her remains in her car.

She can't bring herself to throw it away.

"I probably never will," she said.

JoAnne Klimovich photo
Just days before Evelyn's death, her daughter Ruth, visits with her.

Again, my mom slept through most of Ruth's visit, but opened her eyes slightly right before she was about to leave.

Ruth is the creative, free-spirited one of the siblings.

Dave, the engineer, is thoughtful, analytical and pensive.

Paula, the nurse, is practical and to-the-point.

Rose is all business.

All of them are kind and generous people. We were raised that way.

And we were all devastated by the thought of losing Evelyn, though we all dealt with it in our own ways.

Ruth tried her best to get our mom to talk with her.

"I just kept touching her and hoping she'd wake up," she said.

Ruth, who said she hadn't visited since December 2019, was shocked at how much our mother had deteriorated in that time.

"Mom, Mom, Mom," she said, almost like a toddler trying to get her mother's attention.

Hoping to get a rise from Evelyn, she joked with her.

"At one point I told her that you (JoAnne) were picking on me!"

Finally, she rested her head on the sheets beside Evelyn and whispered, "I love you mama."

Although Evelyn looked at her, she didn't respond, but I know she felt the love that day.

Before Ruth left, I gave her Schenley, a stuffed dog my mother loved, to pass on to her daughter, Violet, who shares the same birthday as Evelyn.

My sisters Paula and Rose didn't make it to visit my mom before she died.

Paula didn't get her travel arrangements made from Tennessee and Rose thought we had more time, they both said later.

Two years later, Ruth still reflects on her visit, the memories still fresh in her mind.

"When I went in, it seemed a lot worse than I thought it was going to be. You weren't saying a lot, and she hardly woke up, probably because of all the meds," she said.

Ruth said she texted our brother and sisters and told them to immediately call or text me because as she said in her text, "this isn't good, call or text her today. Mom is really sick. JoAnne needs us."

"I wished I would have seen her sooner. I was bawling on the way back (to New Jersey)," Ruth said later. "It was worse than I thought. I knew it was bad, and I felt bad for you and for mom."

She told me she was worried about my mental health.

"I know you would have stayed (forever), but mentally this was not good for you," she said. "There was isolation, and you are not one of those people who like isolating. It wouldn't bother me, but you like talking to people. The good thing is the people there knew you. You hear about bad nursing homes, but that one seemed really good."

After Ruth's visit, all signs were from the hospice nurses were that we didn't have much time remaining.

I spent every minute in that blue recliner next to her, only getting up to run – and I mean run – to the bathroom.

I ate all my meals and did my work in that chair. I wasn't budging for anything, not a shower, not a change of clothes or anything else.

Throughout the night, Evelyn would reach for me, and I was there, awake all night to grab her hand and hold it for as long as it took for the pain or a sudden wave of anxiety to pass.

On Thursday, June 4 she slept most of the day and woke up at dinner time to let me feed her a few bites of strawberry ice cream that Cindy from Big Jim's brought us before lapsing back into a sound sleep.

The rabbi stopped by to check on us and asked if I wanted a priest to give my mother the last rites.

I told him that as a devout Catholic, that would mean the world to us.

His kindness overwhelmed me. I was so grateful.

Soon afterward, Father Dan Walsh from Saint Paul Cathedral Parish walked in the door, outfitted in the mandatory gown, face mask and gloves.

I realized that with covid-19 still very much a risk, both the rabbi and Father Dan put themselves at great risk by being there, but they'll never know the comfort they provided at such a horrific time.

Father Dan knows us from Mass at St. Rosalia, which is part of Saint Paul Cathedral.

He sat with me for a few minutes and talked about my mother's dedication to her faith.

He knew how crushing her death would be for me because he'd watched the two of us interact. He knew how inseparable we were and what emptiness I would feel when she was gone.

Though Evelyn never woke, he so carefully and gently placed his hand on the crown of her head and prayed for the Holy Spirit to come upon her. He invited me to place my hand on my mom's head and pray with him.

I sobbed knowing that the end was close.

He read from a prayer book for the Rite of Anointing of The Sick.

When he left, I felt a peacefulness. I hoped Evelyn felt it, too.

But I also had this feeling that I shouldn't leave her side for anything or anybody.

I was right.

The next day, a little after 5 p.m., she coughed.

I was scrolling on my phone but looked up as she struggled for a few breaths.

I think she was trying to tell me something.

I saw the top of her chest stop moving and a slight movement from the bottom of her chest.

Panicked, I called out for an aide, who in turn called a nurse.

She took a few more staggered breaths ... and then her last.

The time was 5:15 p.m.

I remember I screamed and held her hand as workers came running into the room.

I just couldn't let go of her hand. I sat there, squeezing her hand, sobbing uncontrollably as a blur of faces and voices tried to comfort me.

Some hugged me.

Some tried to move me from my mother's side, but I wasn't budging.

There were the sights and sounds of people rushing in and out of the room.

I remember a call being made to the hospice nurse to pronounce her dead.

Two workers who had left for the day at 3 p.m., came back.

When others heard, they came rushing in.

I needed to talk to Perry ... and to my siblings.

I'd call Perry first, then my oldest sister, Rose.

I'm not even sure what I said to Perry through my tears.

My conversation with Rose was short. It's all that I could muster before being overcome by more sobs that made talking impossible.

Rose said she'd call my brother and sisters. She's the big sister who always has been there for us. She learned that role from Evelyn.

After I hung up with her, I sat in the recliner next to Evelyn and cried so hard that my entire body hurt.

She was gone.

But I was still there, still not leaving her side.

Perry later told me he was at home making chili when I called and dropped everything to make the half hour drive to the nursing home.

I met him at the nursing home entrance.

For the first time in three months, we hugged as my tears continued to flow.

He put on a gown, face mask and gloves and we walked to Evelyn's room.

I wanted to give Perry a little time alone with Evelyn. I knew he was hurting. At least I had been with her for the last three months, but he'd been denied that time.

As we walked to her room, one of the aides said Rosie wanted to talk to me. She'd heard about Evelyn and wanted to talk.

I headed down the hall to her room, trying to compose myself along the way.

I needed to be strong for her.

But the minute we saw each other, we both burst into tears.

Her friend was gone, and I know it hurt so badly.

I sat on her bed, and I hugged her for the longest time.

While I tended to Rosie, Perry sat with Evelyn.

He told me later that he said his own goodbye that night to the best mother-in-law that a man could hope for in this life.

He held her hand.

When I walked back into the room, he was sitting next to her bed not saying a word. I knew that he was grieving.

Evelyn, the woman who meant so much to both of us, was gone.

We just sat there for the longest time, staring at her, trying to come to grips with it all.

Our time alone with her abruptly ended when the nurse in charge came by to say they had to prepare my mom for the funeral home.

She said, she didn't think I'd want to be there while they did that and perhaps, we should leave the room for a while.

I really didn't want to leave, but was too weak and too stunned to fight it.

Perry and I went to the nearby courtyard and sat outside in the warm summery air.

It was time for us to become reacquainted after months apart.

We tried to comfort each other. We talked about Evelyn. We shared stories about her. Some were funny.

He loves to tell the story about the time that Evelyn insisted she come along with us when I took him for a colonoscopy.

He said "How many mothers-in-law would want to do that?

"A good one, that's who," he later recalled.

Maybe it was because when she and my dad were in the hospital, he was always there with them without fail.

Maybe it was because she just loved him so much.

When she saw him in the recovery room after the procedure, she said something about how different it was to be looking at him in a hospital bed this time.

Perry loved that she was there with him that day.

On the way back to Evelyn's room the night that she died, I told him that I wanted to spend one more night in the nursing home.

I needed that night to collect my thoughts and begin to grieve in the room where Evelyn lived and died. I didn't want to step away from her room, her bed or her belongings. I wanted one more night there with the memories of her and our time together. Just one more night.

He never questioned me about it.

And as he did for the nearly three months I was quarantined with Evelyn, he understood ... completely.

He always does.

Chapter 9 –

Alone

AND JUST LIKE THAT, THE funeral director came and took Evelyn away.

She was gone from Charles Morris and from my life, but she'd never be gone from my once-strong heart that was now shattered in a thousand pieces.

Perry gave me one last long hug and turned to leave, telling me he'd see me tomorrow at home – our home, the one I'd walked away from in March, the one that seemed just a distant memory to me at this stage.

As I closed the door behind him, shutting out the hallway noises, I thought about all that had happened in this room.

For the first time in nearly three months, I was alone, but not lonely.

I sat down in my chair, grateful for this moment of solitude in this small space where so much had happened.

Seasons changed.

Holidays came and went.

I lost a job, then got it back.

I watched the world outside come to a grinding halt as this virus exacted its cruelty in such a random fashion.

And just now, as life began to regain its former look and feel, Evelyn died.

I felt like I didn't want to move, in part from the exhaustion fueled by the worry and the tears and the utter devastation of watching my mother take her last breath.

Without question, I felt sure that was an image that would remain with me for the rest of my life.

I also felt that my mental health was tenuous at best.

But how could it have been anything else?

First, I thought the lockdown would last two weeks and then it didn't.

Then there was the layoff.

And the breast cancer diagnosis.

And I couldn't get my mother to a doctor because of the pandemic.

I couldn't sleep and when I did sleep it was in my clothes, sitting up in a chair.

I wasn't eating right.

And when my mother died, I felt like a failure who didn't accomplish what I was supposed to do – get Evelyn through this pandemic.

Nevermind that her death really had nothing to do with the pandemic.

On that night, I seemed unable to separate the pandemic from the cancer.

My thought process was cloudy at best.

But I still wasn't ready to admit to anyone but myself that the experience or my mother's death had taken any toll on me.

That would be a sign of weakness.

And that unwillingness to accept that I was hurting, would be one of my greatest mistakes.

On that first night without Evelyn, I didn't want to talk with anyone or see anyone.

That night, as the sun was beginning to set, I gazed out the window, knowing that the next few days would be an emotional roller coaster as I re-entered the outside world and planned Evelyn's funeral.

I paced around the room trying to decide what to do.

I talked to Evelyn off and on that night.

I told her that I never wanted it to end this way and that she was my best friend and best mother ever. I told her that I would always miss her and I wasn't sure what to do without her.

I took off the hat that I'd had on for what seemed like days and changed into a pair of my mom's long black lounge pants and her blue "Golden Girls" T-shirt, which has a photo of the four women who always made us laugh.

I slid on a pair of her warm fuzzy socks.

I guess I felt that wearing her clothes would make me feel closer to her.

I walked into the bathroom, took one look in the mirror and was shocked at how tired and pale I appeared.

Dark smudges of makeup remained below my eyes that still were red and puffy from the hours I'd spent crying.

Though I brushed my teeth and scrubbed my face, my pain still was clearly visible.

I turned on the lamp by my mom's bed—switched to its lowest setting.

As the sun dropped lower in the sky, I could feel the darkness of my mood building.

I looked at my cot and my mom's bed, the one she slept on for four years and two months. Her pillow with the Steelers pillow case still had the indentation where she laid her head. A second pillow was hidden underneath.

Her body pillow covered in zebra print was resting against the wall. Her covers and top sheet were scrunched up near the bottom of the bed.

The call light with the cord coming out from the wall was lying in the middle of the mattress.

That pink stuffed pig of hers peered out from under the covers.

I grabbed my phone from my cot, moved my mom's tray table and climbed into her bed. It made a slight creaking noise.

I pulled the sheet and covers up to my chest and grabbed the bed control that was hanging from the right side on the floor to raise the head of the bed.

I clutched that stuffed animal to my chest as I laid my head on her pillow.

I could smell her on that pillow. She was with me. I could feel her presence.

And then I bawled uncontrollably wanting so desperately to roll back the events of that day. I didn't care if anyone heard me as I sobbed so long and so hard that my face hurt and my eyes burned from the nonstop flood of tears.

I'd rise from the bed and walk around the room, desperately trying to think about what to do next to ease my deep, dark sorrow.

I thought about turning on the television, but decided against it.

I preferred the silence.

Everywhere I looked, I was reminded of how much I wanted my mom to be back with me.

I crawled back into her bed and cried some more.

Finally, exhaustion set in and as I was drifting off to sleep, there was a knock at the door.

It startled me.

I was too weak to get up, so I just quietly told them to, "Come in."

It was Tiniece, one of the nursing assistants. She brought me a white Styrofoam cup filled with ice water. A straw partially covered with white paper stuck out from the top.

She put it on my tray table, then moved toward me, asking if she could give me a hug.

She said she was sorry to hear about "Miss E," her nickname for my mom.

She told me to hit the call button if I needed anything.

What I needed, she didn't have.

I needed my mother.

I spotted the cup my mom last drank from. I wanted to keep it forever.

Next to it were her rosary beads, a box of tissues, her cell phone and the television remote.

A reporter's notebook and pen were there for me to record my thoughts.

I reached for them and wrote a few things about Evelyn's final day.

As I looked around the room, I saw her wheelchair. I spotted all the family photos, including the one of she and my dad on their wedding day.

Now they're both gone.

I buried my head in her pillow and cried some more.

My head and my heart were at odds with each other.

I knew that finally they were happy in heaven together.

But at that moment, I was missing them both so intensely that every inch of my body ached.

At some point, my tears slowed and I just gazed at the ceiling for what might have been hours, thinking random thoughts about Evelyn and life in general.

I believe so deeply in God and the eternal life that waits for us after this one.

I wondered if Evelyn was already in heaven and imagined how joyous her reunion must have been with my dad. I was happy for them.

At one point, I thought, maybe this is how it feels to be a patient in a nursing home.

You're all alone.

You're lying in bed staring at the ceiling and you're just waiting.

You wait for your meals.

You wait to get dressed.

You wait for your medication.

You wait for someone to take you to the bathroom.

You wait for visitors.

And at some point, you wait to die.

After that weighty discussion in my mind, the random, stream-of-consciousness thoughts stopped and I slept.

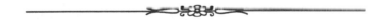

The next morning, I woke up about 7:30 and for a moment wondered if it was all a dream.

But there was no Evelyn.

And as I looked at the table near the door, I saw a breakfast tray with my name on it.

On each of the previous 84 days, there always had been two trays – one for me and one for Evelyn.

Today there was one.

After mindlessly eating a bowl of Rice Krispies and a banana, I crawled out of bed and texted the activities director, Carol, who said she and her assistant, Marcellina, would stop in around 11 a.m. to help me pack up the room.

I put on my mom's bathrobe and went down the hall take a shower.

On my way there, I ran into the nurse on duty who gave me a hug.

I came back to the room to put on some makeup, dry my hair and get dressed.

I'm not sure what was powering me that day as I just went through the motions of doing the things I knew I needed to do before I could leave.

I started going through some of my mom's things.

Carol and her assistant, Marcellina arrived with boxes and a wheeled cart.

Thank God they were there, because the thought of going through my mother's belongings was almost too much for me.

They helped me organize three piles—keep, toss, donate. You could tell they'd done this before.

In between placing items in their proper place, we talked and we cried.

I needed an outfit for my mother to be buried in. They told me to choose a few of Evelyn's favorite clothes and decide later. It was just too much for me to think about today.

Carol and Marcellina have been with us from the first day my mom moved into Charles Morris.

They treat every resident like they are their parent.

They're patient and caring beyond description.

Carol recently told me my time in the nursing home was a blessing for her and Marcellina.

"Your loyalty to Evelyn and all the residents was remarkable," said Carol, whose mother, Carol, was my Aunt Pat's sister.

Finally, we were finished and the room was empty, pretty much devoid of any signs that Evelyn ever lived there.

As I was about to leave, I paused for a few seconds to take it all in.

Her bed and my cot had only a sheet on them.

I looked at the bare windowsill – the place where I had slept more than four years ago. The pictures were all gone. The window was cracked a few inches and the sun was shining.

I closed the door and made what seemed like an arduously long walk out of the building … after 85 days.

We packed my car, which had been parked at the nursing home since I arrived back in March.

Perry moved it once, just to make sure it was still running, and when he didn't return it to the same parking place, there was a little bit of a dust-up among nursing home workers who thought I had left the facility at some point.

I texted Perry and told him I was coming home.

Finally, I was returning to my real life, but I almost forgot what that life looked like.

Driving home that Saturday morning was a surreal experience.

When I slid behind the wheel of my SUV, it was like I was in a stranger's vehicle.

I sat there for a moment, trying to think about how to start the car, put it in gear and go.

Bright sunlight came streaming through the windshield.

I hadn't seen that kind of direct sunlight in so long,

I rolled the window partially down and a warm breeze blew in on me as I drove away, seeing Charles Morris fade away in my rear-view mirror.

As I pulled onto the Parkway East heading toward downtown Pittsburgh, the traffic seemed to be moving so fast.

And I seemed to be moving in slow motion.

I realized that life had continued without me for all those months. The people driving past me had no idea where I had been, what I'd just been through or what I'd lost.

When I arrived home about 25 minutes later, Perry was waiting. He and I unloaded most of my things into our garage, not saying much in the process.

He's never been one to hover over me, so he gave me some space as I walked up two flights of steps and into the bedroom.

I decided to lie down on the bed and rest for a bit.

It was comfortable, yet it felt strange to me.

My phone was ringing and buzzing with text messages.

I wasn't ready to talk to anyone just yet. This time yesterday, Evelyn was still alive, I thought.

I just laid there on the bed in silence.

I was numb.

After a while, I told Perry that I needed to get out of that room and out of the house.

We decided to get something to eat at Coach's, a sports bar not from our house that a friend, Johnny Lee, co-owns.

Johnny had always been so kind to my parents. He'd buy my dad an Iron City Beer and get my mother a bowl of the soup-of-the-day anytime they were there.

Perry ate there often while I was gone.

Although it felt so odd being out around people, I felt comfortable being there that day with someone I knew cared about us.

We sat outside and Johnny greeted me with a big hug.

Perry and I ate and talked, but I don't think I was the best dining companion.

When we went home, I just needed to crawl back into that bed again.

But as I lay there, exhausted – both mentally and physically – sleep still evaded me.

A random thought about Evelyn or my dad would make me cry and just when I thought I was OK, the tears would start again.

I wondered if I would ever stop crying and if I could ever think about them without becoming wildly emotional.

Clutching that little stuffed pig that I'd brought with me from the nursing home, I just stared off into space, occasionally gazing at a photo of Paul and Evelyn that was nearby.

I remember when they went to have that photo taken. They made up a story about where they were going that day. They went to a professional studio and we each received an 8x10 photo as a Christmas present.

I'm so glad they did.

The next morning, I got up and moved around the house from which I'd been absent for so long.

After months of living in that tiny room with Evelyn, our house seemed so enormous.

Those first few days, Perry and I seemed like two strangers living in this big house.

We wanted to be there to comfort each other and he did comfort me, but we wanted to give each other the time and space to readjust to our living situation.

After all, for nearly three months, we'd been living separate lives.

And now we were both grieving.

I realized that all of this was difficult for him, too.

Even before the lockdown, I wasn't home very much and neither was he.

In addition to working full time, for 16 ½ years, I was always off taking care of my parents and now suddenly I was going to be home more than ever before.

Perry was devoted to teaching his students and coaching basketball, which took him away from home both day and many nights.

It would be a period of adjustment for both of us.

There were times when I felt I was in a stranger's house.

Many things looked new to me.

There were things I forgot I had.

There were clothes that I'd left behind and put out of my mind.

But then there were things in the same place where I had left them months before.

Through it all, my mind kept returning to Charles Morris and all that occurred there.

I missed it and I missed my Charles Morris family.

That morning, I wrote a Facebook post about my experience. Here's an excerpt:

> *My mother, my best friend, Evelyn died. For those of you who know me know she and I were more than mother and daughter. We were pretty much inseparable. We completed each other.*
>
> *I took her to church every week at St. Rosalia in Greenfield. We had many lunches and dinners at Big Jim's Restaurant in the Run. Her favorite item on the menu? Italian Wedding Soup.*
>
> *We gambled at the Rivers Casino and ate at Mineo's Pizza in Squirrel Hill.*

We watched many, many Pirates games.

I had been caring for her for 16 and ½ years since she had a stroke on Jan. 2, 2004, leaving her paralyzed on the left side. But she didn't let that stop her from living her life. I would help her into her wheelchair, roll her out to my car and put her in the passenger seat.

She was my true co-pilot. We talked about everything and I mean everything.

She was the best listener and often gave me wardrobe advice.

My mother enjoyed chocolate chip cookies and strawberry ice cream. She liked to sleep in and play bingo. Everyone loved her.

Cancer came and took her away from me.

I was there, holding her hand. I wanted to be there because I didn't want her to be afraid. There is a special bond between mother and child. She watched me take my first breath and I watched her take her last.

She is with my dad, Paul, who died five years ago today. He is taking care of her now. I am sure he missed her.

Their love spanned 66 years.

Evelyn taught her children about love. She always told me "Treat others the way you want to be treated, and if you are nice to people, they will be nice to you."

I prayed to God to give me the strength to get through the next few days and the days that came after as I learned to live life without Evelyn at my side.

As I was posting this message, my phone buzzed. It was a text from Rosie's daughter-in-law to see how I was doing. She and Bobby wanted to see us, so Perry and I decided to meet them for pizza at Mineo's, one of the takeout places that kept us going during the lockdown at Charles Morris.

After months of being completely shut down, restaurants were beginning to open up for indoor dining, but at a reduced capacity.

Once seated at Mineos, Rosie's family thanked me for checking on her while I was in quarantine.

I felt good to be there with people I loved so much, but there was an uneasiness about being out in public. I'd been cut off from the world for so long, I realized this was going to take some time.

I ate a few slices of plain pizza and drank a tall glass of Grey Goose vodka with coke.

I thought the alcohol might help me get some rest when we went home that night.

It didn't work.

I found that nothing on this earth, not even a shot of good vodka, could relax me enough to let me get a good night's sleep.

Chapter 10 –

Life After Evelyn

AFTER A WEEKEND OF SLEEPLESS nights intermingled with a steady barrage of conversations, texts and phone calls, it was Monday morning.

While my brother and sisters packed and made travel plans to head to Pittsburgh, Perry and I got ready to meet with the funeral director, our priest and the cadre of others involved in Evelyn's funeral.

As a family, we decided the viewing would be Thursday and Friday and the funeral on Saturday, a week and a day after Evelyn died.

It gave me a little time to breathe, and I was grateful for that.

Earlier that first morning, I sat down to begin the most difficult writing assignment of my life – my mother's obituary.

I sat there staring at my blank computer screen and asked myself, "How on earth can I do this?"

How do you sum up 93 years of unconditional loving, of bringing five kids into this life and teaching them to be good people in a world where goodness sometimes does not prevail?

I wrote and revised, then started over again and again, frustrated by my inability to write my mother's story.

Words seemed inadequate.

Through a seemingly endless stream of tears running down my face, I tried again and again to capture her life and her spirit. I tried to convey what a gift this tiny God-fearing, courageous woman had been to each of us.

I abandoned the idea of writing great prose and decided to make it simple and straightforward, much like my mom. Just the facts with a little bit of the heart and soul of Evelyn's amazing life interspersed for good measure.

Here's an excerpt:

Our beloved mother, Evelyn (D'Antonio) Klimovich, 93, a native of Bellevue, longtime resident of Greenfield and then Schenley Gardens in Oakland and most recently at Charles Morris Nursing and Rehabilitation Center in Squirrel Hill, left this earth for heaven to join her husband of 66 years, Paul. She will be buried on Saturday, June 13, exactly five years to the day that he was buried.

They will be together again.

During her life, Evelyn overcame many obstacles. Her father left the family when she was a child. She endured scarlet fever at a young age and could only see out of one eye. She was paralyzed by a stroke 16 years ago. But she never let those challenges stop her from living a full life with Paul. They dedicated their lives to their children, St. Rosalia Church and the community of Greenfield.

There were times she only had $20 for the week to buy groceries. She would plan meals to accommodate everyone's schedule. Her homemade meat ravioli was the best.

With only one car, she often took the bus to attend her children's sports activities. But she never complained. She made it work because there was always plenty of love.

Even when she wasn't feeling well because of the cancer, she would look out the window and say, "It looks nice outside, can we go out?" She accepted everyone and appreciated those who cared for her and often told them that.

Evelyn enjoyed many lunches and dinners at her favorite restaurant, Big Jim's in the Run, where they treated her like royalty, and outings to the Rivers Casino on the North Side, where the quarter slots were her favorite. She loved playing bingo and watching Pirates baseball on television. She was a true fan and spent many afternoons at PNC Park, despite using a wheelchair. She also attended Steelers and Pitt football games and even one Penguins game – her first at the age of 92.

The family would like to extend a heartfelt thank-you to all of the staff at Charles Morris Nursing and Rehabilitation Center in Squirrel Hill, where Evelyn lived since April 2016, as well as Schenley Gardens in Oakland, where the couple resided for many years.

In lieu of flowers, the family suggests donations in her memory to the Jewish Association on Aging for the Activities Department at Charles Morris Nursing and Rehabilitation Center or, the next time you visit Big Jim's, order a cup of the Italian wedding soup in her memory.

Later that day, Perry and I went to Kanai Funeral Home in Greenfield to begin the process of planning Evelyn's farewell.

When we walked in the door, I immediately was transported back to overwhelming sadness of my dad's funeral.

But there were differences.

This time there was talk about covid-19.

Masks would be required. Limits on the number of people inside the funeral parlor at any given time would be imposed. Hugging and handshakes were not encouraged.

All signs of the new world in which we were living.

In addition to keeping everyone safe from covid, we had a list of tasks I knew we needed to complete that day.

There was so much to think about, and I wanted so desperately for everything to be perfect, just the way Evelyn would have envisioned it.

There would be no second chances, no "do overs."

The first order of business?

Selecting a casket.

We walked across the street to another building where a room full of pieces of caskets of all sizes and colors were displayed along a wall.

It was a bizarre and unsettling image, to say the least. When planning my dad's funeral, we browsed a catalog of caskets to select one.

Suddenly, the finality of what we were doing shook me to my core.

The tears came heavy and hard as I listened as the funeral director say his father, who was retired, planned to be part of the funeral out of respect for our family.

How incredibly kind, I told him.

But that's what Greenfield people do. They take care of each other.

Evelyn would be so flattered.

It might sound a little silly, but I also think Evelyn would have been pleased with the blue casket that we chose for her. She loved anything blue and always gravitated toward it when I took her shopping.

From the box of her belongings that I carried from the nursing home, I tried to carry on that blue theme by pulling out a baby blue sweater, a royal blue turtleneck, her favorite silver necklace with a small stone that she got in a giveaway at the casino, the bracelet she loved with dice dangling from it and her rosary beads. That leopard print blanket that she treasured would cover her legs.

I also handed the funeral director a bra, a brief, a pair of her warm fuzzy socks and her favorite comfortable black shoes.

I needed to find a good photo for the hairdresser to use.

Her hair would have to look perfect. That would be important to my mom.

The next hour or so quickly became a blur of discussions about the details of the three days earmarked to honor Evelyn. There was talk of flowers and pallbearers and the Mass and the graveside services.

It all seemed to fall into place with relative ease with the help of the funeral director, whose calm demeanor and experience in dealing with the details of death helped guide us through this most unpleasant experience.

Our next stop was my friend Jane's house where we met with Father Dan, just days after he'd given my mom the last rites.

We talked about Evelyn and her deep, abiding faith. We talked about the Mass and how it would play out. By far, this would be the most important part of the day for Evelyn.

Later, Jane and I made several photo boards with snapshots of my mom when she was a young woman, a new wife and mother and a doting grandmother.

In some of the photos, she sat smiling in front of a slot machine.

There were photos with her grandchildren, several with my dad and some with my siblings and me. Others showed her with Rosie and the workers from Charles Morris and Schenley Gardens who became her friends.

The photos and the memories they elicited made me smile for the first time in days.

I thought about what they represented.

A life in photos.

Nine decades.

A perfect love story between two people whose lives were never easy, but whose undying devotion to each other and to the family they created never waned for a second.

That night, with my "to do" list completed, I went home and once again retreated to the bedroom where I just sat collapsed on my bed and cried.

For that day, my work was done.

But I knew the toughest days were yet to come.

The six days that passed between Evelyn's death and the first day of the funeral home viewing was the longest period I had been separated from her in more than 16 years.

When I saw her in that casket for the first time, it was more jarring than I could have ever imagined.

Though I think she looked beautiful and peaceful, I wasn't ready for the goodbyes that were about to come.

I tried to focus on the floral displays that encircled her casket and the pastel drawing of my parents' wedding photo sitting nearby on an easel.

A candle with Evelyn's photo was illuminated in front of the casket.

A cushioned kneeler was placed close by for people to pray.

As friends and family filed into the room, I cried as they told stories about my mom, although I admit that I didn't hear every word because of their face masks.

"She looks so nice," so many said.

"You know she loved you so much," others told me.

So many of those who came tried to comfort me as I stood there before my mother's casket crying my eyes out.

People hugged me even though they knew they shouldn't because of the virus.

I hated this pandemic.

I wanted to hug everyone.

I wanted to savor every word and outpouring of love for Evelyn that was spoken.

But those masks and these circumstances prevented that.

I regret that I don't remember all who came or recall every gesture of kindness.

There were people from Charles Morris, from Schenley Gardens, old neighbors, friends of mine and even a friend of my brother who drove in from Ohio.

I hated that so many people who wanted to come to pay their respects couldn't for fear they might contract the dreaded virus that still was killing people despite the fact most of Pennsylvania was reopening for business that same week.

So many of my mom and dad's elderly friends had been holed up in their homes since spring, fearful of what might happen to them if they were out in a crowd.

They came out for my dad, and I knew they would have come for my mom.

I know that Evelyn wouldn't have wanted them to take that chance and I certainly didn't either, but in some ways, I felt Evelyn was cheated out of the tribute she so richly deserved after living a life of service to so many.

At the end of each of the two days of visitation, when it was time to go home, I shuddered at the thought of leaving Evelyn alone all night at the funeral parlor.

It was something that I promised I would never do.

On the day of the funeral, I got out of bed, only because it was what my mom would have done.

I barely had the strength to move.

It was a beautiful, clear day outside, but I failed to see any beauty in it.

Fran Sissel Wyner photo
JoAnne kneels at her mother's casket on the day of her funeral.

I put on a black and white dress, black Mary Jane heels, Evelyn's red blazer and a big black hat with a huge flower and polka dot trim. I grabbed a pair of white gloves.

We arrived at the funeral home at 9 a.m. The mass was at 10 a.m.

At 9:30, we were invited to say our final good-bye.

Earlier, I'd taken care of some business with the funeral director.

Knowing this funeral marked the last time I would ever see my mother, I wanted to have a few final and private words with her.

Just as I had done for my dad, I found the strength to reach into my purse and pull out a piece of paper and a pen.

Tears streamed down my face as I wrote my last-ever note to my mom.

Over the years, I'd written her so many notes, some funny, all heartfelt. One year, on my birthday, I'd even sent her a card thanking her for giving birth to me.

On this day, I folded the note and asked the funeral director to place it in my mom's right hand, her good hand.

"I love you Evelyn, my mother, my best friend," I wrote. "I know you and dad will take care of each other in heaven."

I drew a heart below the words.

I knew she was embraced by the loving arms of my dad. They were dancing together, once again as they had in that West View dance hall more than 60 years ago when they first met.

The funeral director approached, asking if I wanted my mom's wedding band, engagement ring and anniversary band. I said, "no."

"Yes, she wants the rings," my sister Paula stepped in to say.

I thought the rings belonged with my mother for eternity. They represented the love my dad had for my mom.

She often talked about how nice the diamonds looked after so long.

"They've gone through everything over the years, and they still shine," she would say.

In recent years, the rings were on her right hand because her left hand was clenched from the stroke.

But Paula insisted I take the rings as a keepsake for all that I did for Evelyn and because she said she would want me to have them.

I relented after realizing that having those rings would provide a lasting connection to her.

To this day, I wear them – much too tiny for my ring finger – on my right pinkie.

I remember walking into our church that day and seeing all of the people wearing masks and socially distanced.

It seemed wrong on so many levels that at a time when people were coming together to comfort each other, that they should be forced apart.

Again, the turnout was lower than it might have been if it hadn't been for the pandemic. But still, there were so many who cast their fears aside to attend the Mass, I'm sure because Evelyn had been such a faithful servant of the church for so many years.

I sat in the front row with Perry, my sister, Rose and her boyfriend, Mark.

Father Dan gave a wonderful homily about my mom and the fact that her commitment to the church and attending Mass never waned because she was confined to a wheelchair.

He talked about her as a perfect example of living a life of faith.

My brother stepped before those assembled to deliver the eulogy that our family had written together.

Unlike me, Dave doesn't wear his heart on his sleeve. He's so kind and so generous, but he's not emotional as I am so often.

But on this day, even he said he found himself choked up a few times as he spoke about Evelyn and Paul and the wonderful lives they had given all of us.

I couldn't have done it. I don't know how he made it through.

Here is an excerpt from it:

You can't pick your parents.

Usually, when you hear someone say something along those lines, he or she is complaining.

Not so with my sisters and me. There's no way that, given the choice, we could have been blessed with better parents than Paul and Evelyn.

As many of you will recall, five years ago, actually five years ago to this day ... we laid our dad, Paul Klimovich, to rest. That's pretty amazing when you think about it. Whether by fate, the hand of Divine Providence, or sheer coincidence, this U.S. Army veteran of the Normandy landings went to his heavenly reward on June 6, 2015. Evelyn's last words to Paul at the funeral home were: "See you later, Buddy." And now, I am sure they are together again.

Like Paul, Evelyn faced many challenges growing up in the lean years of the Great Depression. Both could have emerged from these tough experiences as hardened or fearful people. Instead, they became optimistic, generous, and loving, determined to make life much easier for their children, whatever sacrifices it took.

Tending to the daily needs of five pretty typical youngsters could wear down the hardiest soul, but somehow Evelyn mustered the energy and good humor to keep the confusion in some semblance of order. When she had the twins, she didn't even know until the day they were born. Paul even delivered one of them at home, then the other was born in the hospital – I don't know which, I was three at the time, but you could read about it, it was in all the papers. Still, Evelyn kept everything under control.

Money was tight, but she somehow found a way to keep us well-fed, healthy, and decently clothed ... In large part through her constant vigilance, we all got good educations, and thus were able to make better lives for ourselves, and later for our own children.

That would have been more than enough to merit Evelyn star status as a parent, but she somehow, miraculously, found the time and energy to do so much more. Unfazed by her heavy load of daily domestic duties, she also was a tireless worker at parish and community events. It was important to her that she, and oftentimes Dad, attended all her kids' activities. Even when dad had the family car at work, and we were engaged in sports or school activities, she often braved long bus rides to enjoy watching us perform, a true proud parent. She and Dad were given a trophy for attending all of JoAnne's CYO basketball games when Jo was a senior, and she said it was the first trophy she had ever received. For a lot of things, Mom was in the background, but we always knew she was there supporting us.

Rather than looking for a well-deserved breather and putting her feet up for a spell, she instead chose to be in perpetual motion, always doing things for others. As numerous relatives, friends, and neighbors can attest, they always could count on being welcomed by Evelyn with an open door and at the very least a full table of cookies at 4217 Stanley Street, any time, any day.

The examples that Evelyn and Paul set for us, their children, were crystal clear, and made indelible marks on us all. Honesty. Hard work. Generosity. Love of neighbor and family. Faith. Their lives started in the era of KDKA radio and landline phones on party lines, all the way through to cell phones, GPS, and the Internet, but they always adjusted well.

When she was incapacitated by a stroke 16 ½ years ago, her sudden shift from perpetual motion to forced inaction was a tough transition. Still, she dealt with a highly unfortunate situation as best she could, always eager to chat with visitors, always appreciative of those who'd take the time to share a memory or a laugh.

Today she also pays her final goodbye to the parish church that she loved and served so much in her lifetime, and which she insisted on attending regularly, even though I'm sure she could have gotten special dispensation for her lack of mobility. You won't see her wheelchair parked in the front pew, but she will still be here, we guarantee you that.

As Dave finished, I looked to my left and broke down when I didn't see her there in the front row in her wheelchair.

That was her spot. But not anymore.

As we left the church, the funeral director handed me a small, black velvet pouch with my mother's rings inside.

I clutched them knowing full well that at some point, this would be one of the few tangible items that I would have with which to remember her.

We went to our cars for the short drive to the cemetery where there were graveside services with more sad and prayerful goodbyes and tributes.

The family that Paul and Evelyn built encircled her casket that day – the kids and the grandkids there to say their farewells.

It is a big family, a family that Evelyn thought she might never have after Paul Jr. died so many years earlier. It was all she ever wanted, and, in the end, she got it all and then some.

On that day, we all clung to each other in a way that Evelyn would have wanted. Sure, there were tears, but we found comfort in each other. I was so glad to have them all there.

With Perry at my side, I cried throughout the service, dreading the end when we would have to leave.

Finally, the funeral director told us it was time for us to return to our cars.

I stared at the casket, not wanting to move.

I walked slowly past. I stopped for a few minutes, clutching a box of Kleenex in my right hand and placing my left hand on the casket.

I couldn't leave her, I thought.

But then, I looked to the sky and remembered that she's with my dad. He'll take care of her now. They made that promise to each other a long time ago.. And I made good on my promise to him.

Time for you to take over, Paul, I thought as I walked away.

Chapter 11 –

Left Behind

DAYS AFTER WE BURIED EVELYN, the family and friends who gathered in her honor, who celebrated her and told and retold stories of her remarkable life, were gone, returning to their homes and their lives.

When all was said and done, I was left behind in Pittsburgh, struggling to not only grieve, but also reconnect to my life, the one I'd walked away from three months before, a life now missing one crucial element – my mother.

Sleep still seemed out of the question on most nights as I tossed and turned and stared at the stark white ceiling of our bedroom for hours until I knew the location of every crack and crevice.

I wanted so desperately to rest, but my mind wouldn't shut down long enough to permit it. The more I tried to calm myself and sleep, the more anxious I became.

Though I had plenty of people in my life – good people who cared for me – I felt incredibly lonely.

No one understood what I was feeling.

No one had an inkling of what I'd been through.

The depression that came with my loneliness was like a 2-ton weight around my neck.

I wanted to pull myself out of this. I didn't like this feeling of slogging through the days with no energy and no interest in anything around me.

I knew other people who'd lost parents, but they didn't seem to be crippled by it in the same way that I was.

But no one had a relationship with their mother like I had with Evelyn, I told myself.

No one suffered the loss that I suffered when she died.

Work had always been my salvation. A good day at the office made my mood soar.

I loved meeting people and writing stories about their lives.

Maybe I'd feel better when I got back to it.

Although the Trib staff was back in the office in early June for the first time since March, the president of the company decided that, as an added measure of protection, I'd need to quarantine for 21 days before returning.

For nearly three months I'd been locked up in a nursing home, which across the nation had become hotbeds for covid-19 infections due to their vulnerable populations. After leaving the nursing home, I was out in crowds for days, first for my mother's viewing and then for her funeral, both settings viewed by experts as possible "super spreader" events if someone attending was sick or didn't comply with masking or other safety rules in place.

My quarantine was necessary to protect my co-workers who were returning to the office for the first time in months with legitimate concerns about their health and the safety of their families.

The ground rules were clear.

I could report stories from my house, but couldn't go out to interview anyone.

Another period of isolation.

I was right back where I'd started – locked up, doing my job from the confines of one small room, only this time it was in the bedroom of our house.

I wasn't really sure how I felt about the additional time in quarantine.

I guess it didn't really matter to me where I worked because regardless of where I was, I'd still be sad and overwhelmed by just about everything in my life.

In some ways, I'd actually been dreading those first days back in the office where people undoubtedly would ask me about my time away.

Reporters ask questions. That's what they're trained to do and I knew that's exactly what they'd do when I walked back into the newsroom.

I know they'd mean well and they'd want to be supportive, but I didn't want to relive the past three months.

For the three weeks of my latest quarantine, I essentially lived in that bedroom, seldom coming out for anything or anyone.

I set up a small office in the corner of the room.

Perry, who was still working from home most days, would come and gently knock on the door every now and then.

"Are you OK," he'd ask.

Sometimes, he'd say, "Hey, I'm making myself something to eat, can I get something for you?"

I couldn't even decide most days if I wanted to eat.

"I'm fine," I'd tell him, not engaging in much conversation with him even though we were living in the same house.

We were like strangers living under one roof.

It had been so long since we'd been together, I don't think either one of us knew quite what to do.

———————————————◦⋈◦———————————————

It was June and everything outside was starting to spring to life as it does after a long winter in Western Pennsylvania. Trees were in full bloom and people in our neighborhood were planting flowers and readying their homes for summer.

I didn't care about that, either.

It could have been gray and snowing or raining buckets. The outside world seemed irrelevant to me.

I just stared out the second-floor window and tried to muster some enthusiasm for something … anything.

Every now and then, I'd get a text from some well-meaning person in my life – a friend, a family member, a co-worker.

Sometimes I'd acknowledge them. More often I wouldn't.

Through it all, I know that Perry was worried about me, but he continued to give me space, not pushing me to do anything or go anywhere, which I greatly appreciated.

If he had pushed, I know I would have pushed back and the last thing that I needed was any conflict with him. He'd been so good to me, always there for me, but I had a hard time even expressing that emotion.

After Evelyn's funeral, as I sat at home writing thank-you notes, I wrote one to him.

I know that to some people, that seems odd.

As a writer, it seemed the best way to let him know how I felt.

But even that note probably lacked my true feelings of gratitude for all that he had done.

On a small white Hallmark card with a pink rose and a gold-embossed message on the front saying, "Thank you for your expression of sympathy," I wrote,

———————⋯⋯⋯———————

June 2020

Perry –

Little did we realize that the words "in sickness and in health" would apply to my parents and not each other.

I know I haven't told you often but I appreciate all you did for Paul and Evelyn. You spent more time with them than their own children (except for me of course!)

The past few months, I would not have made it through without you – from bringing us food to getting me a new phone to picking up my computer. I won't forget that. You saw the bond that Evelyn and I had and you were part of that because you loved both of us.

Love you,

JoAnne

While I struggled to just get out of bed most days, the world around me was moving on to whatever came next.

Businesses that survived the shutdowns mandated during the early days of the pandemic were reopening under the governor's latest order.

People were still wary, but most were beginning to feel some hope that an end might be in sight.

Although my co-workers were back to work in June, I'd be home until early July while I completed my quarantine.

I heard from a few colleagues who reached out to me about the anxiety some had about going back out into the world again – completely understandable considering all that had happened in the last few months.

Still others, weary of working at home in isolation, were ready to go back in the office among people again.

I learned about the measures the company was taking to protect employees – in addition to a mask mandate, protective barriers were being erected between work spaces, kits with masks and antibacterial gels being given to every employee, temperature checks would be required at the start of every workday and a schedule of cleaning of our offices throughout the day would be strictly enforced.

It seemed that everything and anything that could be done was being done to keep everyone safe.

It also became very evident that life never would be the same for any of us because of this virus and we all needed to find a way to adapt, which of course, was much easier said than done.

I longed for the old days when everything seemed so much simpler, so much safer, those days when Evelyn was right here by my side.

On most days during my quarantine, the best part of my day came at the end when I could crawl into my bed.

I just wanted the days to end.

But night brought me no respite from my sadness.

My dreams all revolved around Evelyn.

They were so hauntingly vivid. I remembered every detail when I woke each morning.

Often, I'd dream about Evelyn in the one place where we both felt a sense of peace and comfort – our church.

In one dream, she suddenly stood up at the altar and casually walked down some nearby steps. I rejoiced at the miracle of it all, but when I awoke, the reality of her 16 ½ years in a wheelchair quickly returned.

In another dream, I went to the nursing home after work and her room was empty. Panicked, I ran from room to room and floor to floor, frantically searching for her, screaming her name, though no one answered. Finally, I found her in another distant room where she'd been moved. In an act of pure cruelty, no one told either of us about the move.

One of the dreams repeated an all-too-familiar scene.

I'd be taking her somewhere in my car and she'd turn to me and say, "If it wasn't for you, I wouldn't go anywhere. I don't know what I would do without you."

Each time, I'd wake up and realize that it was a dream.

I had no choice but to learn how to live without her.

Finally, my quarantine was over on the Fourth of July and although I felt anything but festive, Perry and I went to a high school graduation party, only staying for a bit to wish the guest of honor good luck before moving on to Bobby and Frani's house for a cookout.

It was surreal to be outside among people again, and the day proved to be a blur of people all showing incredible kindness to me, offering hugs and words of praise about how I'd cared for Evelyn.

On that day, it seemed that everyone had an opinion about how to handle my re-entry into the "real world."

They all came at me, spouting words of advice. My head was spinning.

Do something for yourself, they said.

Take a vacation.

Spend all day at the pool.

Make Evelyn's homemade spaghetti.

Though everyone meant well, none of their suggestions elicited any spark of interest in me.

How could I take a vacation when a trip to the dentist or Salon Bernabo or the eye doctor reduced me to tears because I had been there with Evelyn at one time or another.

Her face, her smile, her laugh were everywhere.

Her imprint was on every facet of my life.

Not a day passed without spontaneous outbursts of tears that I couldn't control.

My grief was my constant companion, robbing me of the ability to enjoy anything or anyone.

Finally in early July, I got the go ahead to return to the office and in-person interviews.

That first morning, I got up and carefully pulled together an outfit, something I didn't have to think about for months, except for the few days of Evelyn's viewing and funeral.

It felt odd to be outside, driving my car around the city and interacting with people face to face.

The city streets still seemed empty compared to what they had been in the days before the pandemic.

"Closed" signs hung from the doors of businesses I feared might never reopen.

Patrons were sparse inside the businesses that were open.

And no one went anywhere without those ubiquitous masks.

As I stepped outside that day, I hoped it was my first step toward some kind of normalcy, whatever that meant.

My first in-person interview was at a local brewery and while I was nervous for some inexplicable reason, the day went off without a hitch.

It felt good.

I was back at it.

Maybe this was what I needed.

The next day, I was starting to get back into a routine. Talking to my editors, making calls, doing interviews.

The grief was still with me, but the work gave me a break from it.

Not long after, Big Jim's hosted a "Wedding Soup Day" in memory of Evelyn.

Every person picking up a "to-go" order received a cup of soup courtesy of Jennifer Bertetto, the president of my company, who'd also provided laminated copies of my mom's obituary so that everyone who received the soup could read her story.

Perry and I spent most of the day at Big Jim's greeting customers. I wore Evelyn's houndstooth blazer over a black dress with black heels.

On that day, there was happiness and laughter as we remembered this incredible little woman who touched so many lives in so many ways.

But my happiness was short-lived.

Soon came the news that cases of covid-19 were surging again, causing the governor to place new "mitigation" orders in place in some areas – many in southwestern Pennsylvania – where the numbers were climbing at an alarming rate.

The order stated that "all businesses are required to conduct their operations in whole or in part remotely through individual teleworking."

"When teleworking is not possible, employees may conduct in-person business operations, provided that the business comply with all aspects of the building safety order and the masking order."

No one was really quite sure what all this meant. Were we back at home? Or could we continue to work at the office?

That night, calls went out from the editors to the entire staff explaining the governor's latest move.

We were given the option of working from home or working at the office.

Most people opted to work from home.

Some had gotten comfortable with remote work and wanted to continue it.

Some felt safer at home, though reporters and photographers continued to go out into the public to do their jobs.

After only a few weeks of being back to our new normal, our buildings would once again be empty, except for managers and a few staffers who'd stop in now and again.

And for the next 11 months, they would remain mostly empty while we all wondered when or if life would ever return to what it had been.

I didn't know what to think or what to do.

I chose to stay at home, once again retreating to that small corner of my upstairs bedroom where my already shaky mental state would become even more frail in the coming weeks and months.

In mid-August, about two months after Evelyn's funeral, Sue, my executive editor, called to discuss the story that we had been kicking around regarding my time in lockdown with my mother.

A few days later, we met in her office with a couple of other editors to talk about it.

I felt comfortable with this group.

We'd all worked together for quite a while.

I was given the chance to do the meeting via computer, but I decided that I'd like to meet face-to-face.

The Trib building was eerily empty that day.

It was the first time since March that I'd stepped inside.

The days that I'd worked after my three-week quarantine were jam-packed with interviews and time out on the road, so I never actually made it back into the office.

I'd written my stories from home, probably not the best idea, given that I had spent so much time there being so miserable and sad.

Everything on my desk was where I'd left it when I raced out the door that day months earlier.

Papers were undisturbed. My sweater still hung on the back of my chair.

It was as if I'd just left the day before, not six months ago.

We held the meeting in Sue's office, all of us masked and socially distanced.

As soon as Sue began talking about the possibility of doing the story, the tears came and wouldn't stop.

I sat there crying, barely able to talk, barely able to answer any questions.

They tried to comfort me, but there were no words that could ease my pain. The more we talked, the worse it got.

They all talked, but I'm not even sure I was processing what they were saying.

It was almost as if the room was spinning out of control with indistinguishable sounds and voices playing in the background.

I didn't say it, but in the back of my mind, I wasn't willing to commit to seeing this story published.

I didn't know if I could go through with it.

I told them I was worried about protecting the people at Charles Morris.

But Charles Morris administrators had cleared my stay there with their legal department. They had their board of directors sign off on it and asked me to sign the necessary waivers.

So my editors questioned who I was trying to protect at Charles Morris? Was there something else that was stopping me?

I don't know, but I guess I was worried that there might have been some other son or daughter who would read the story and wonder why they weren't allowed to stay with their parent.

The people at Charles Morris gave me a once-in-a-lifetime gift and I didn't want to cause any problems for them.

In reality, I guess there weren't too many other sons and daughters who would have done what I did.

Maybe on some level, I just didn't want to do the story because I didn't want to relive all of it again. Truly, I'm not sure what I was thinking.

Sue stopped the meeting and said that I should take some time to think about it. We could get together later to discuss it again, she said.

But when we met a second time weeks later, the results were the same.

I may have cried harder than I did the first time.

They were patient, handing me Kleenex and offering words of comfort.

They asked again if I wanted to do the story.

I said I did.

With that said. Sue asked if I felt like I wanted to file a rough draft of a story with my editor, Ben.

I agreed.

In September, I sent Ben what was essentially a list of my journal entries from the nursing home that was more than 12,000 words – in the newspaper world a length considered to be gargantuan.

I also had more than 1,200 photos taken at the nursing home and archival photos of my mom, my family and me.

In total, it was enough to fill an entire newspaper. None of it was in any particular order and certainly not in any shape to be published anywhere.

Again, I'm not sure what I was thinking.

Maybe I wasn't.

Maybe I thought if I turned in this mammoth chunk of work that clearly wasn't ready for publication that nobody would have to the time or the patience to edit it and they would all just forget about it.

I don't know. My mind was awash in thoughts of sorrow and despondency.

Later, Sue told me that she didn't want to give up on me or the story that she believed would resonate with our readers.

I remember her telling me that, "sooner or later, we all face the issue of dealing with aging parents and eventually, we all face the issue of losing them."

And this was a once-in-a-lifetime opportunity, not only as a journalist, but also as a daughter to let them join you in your experience as you said goodbye to your mother under the most unique and moving circumstances imaginable.

Writing this story might even prove cathartic, she told me.

But, at the same time, she was mindful of my deep grief and told me that if I didn't want to do the story, she would respect that and move on.

After several failed meetings in which I spent most of the time crying, Sue again called for a break.

What I didn't know is that Sue had decided to take those journal entries home and lock herself in her home office off and on for weeks to edit them and write a narrative that would link all of them together to form the beautiful story of my time in quarantine with my mother.

I also didn't know that my other colleagues, visual editor Sean Stipp and designer Melanie Wass, spent days sorting through my mountain of photos, whittling them down to a workable photographic journey through my time in lockdown with Evelyn.

All of this happened without my knowledge, as my grieving continued.

They did what I couldn't.

Later, Sue would jokingly refer to the effort as, "Team JoAnne."

When Sue told me about "Team JoAnne" I smiled, recalling the Big Jim's staff— Heather, Brandy, Natalie, Scott, Karen and Cindy – were all on Team Evelyn." One waitress named Toni was "Team JoAnne."

My mother loved every minute of that and so did I.

Sue told me that when she finished her first draft of my story, she showed it to several of the guys on our staff – all hardened veterans of this business – and all of them were clearly moved by it.

Near the end of the process, just weeks prior to publication, Sean produced a video that he asked me to narrate with a script he had written.

Just the two of us, alone in the newspaper's video studio, I tried again and again, but I just couldn't get through it. Each time, I'd begin to speak and then break down in tears.

So Sean switched gears, coming up with a very short script that required me to say just a few words while images of Evelyn and me flashed on the screen.

Despite all of that, in the finished product, you can still hear my voice cracking as I speak about my mother.

I should have felt good about all of these people doing all of this on my behalf, but what I really felt was incredible, almost crippling anxiety.

I still wasn't sure that I wanted this story to be published.

The thought of it made me sick.

By October, the depth of my depression and grief was so great that I was beginning to admit to myself that I probably needed some help to break free of it.

Good friends were encouraging to me to see a therapist, an idea that I initially rejected.

One of those was Patti Banze, a best friend from high school. Patti knows me better than I know myself. She knew I was hurting.

"Your emotions may be more intense than most other people, which makes grief or anything traumatic or emotional a lot more intense and takes a lot longer to heal," Patti said.

In my mind, I felt there was a stigma attached to therapy.

I never wanted to be viewed as being needy or weak – you know that old saying about never letting them see you cry. But I do cry a lot, probably more than most people, so I guess I am very conflicted in that area.

But by this time, I think I realized that my emotional state was not great, so I agreed to reach out to my company's Employee Assistance Program, which offers free, anonymous counseling sessions.

The anonymity was important. I didn't want anyone knowing what I was doing. I think I felt shame, which I now know was ridiculous, not to mention harmful.

My first hour-long session was Oct. 13 at an office in Mt. Lebanon, not far from my house in the South Hills of Pittsburgh.

It was just over five months after Evelyn died.

By this time, my grief was engulfing me on some days.

The therapist was a kind man who listened intently as I spoke about Evelyn and Paul and my time at Charles Morris.

I talked about not having my brother and sisters nearby and my apprehension about publishing a story about my time in lockdown.

To be honest, I spent most of every session just crying.

I think I repeated myself a lot.

I probably wasn't the easiest person to counsel because I didn't give up a lot of information.

I did say some things that I hadn't said to anyone else, so in that respect, I suppose it was good, but it didn't help.

Maybe I wasn't ready for the help.

Maybe he wasn't the right therapist for me.

A therapist needs to understand the situation that the person he or she is dealing with has been through and I felt this person definitely did not understand what I had been through or what I saw at the nursing home.

Of course, how many people have gone through what I went through?

He told me to do things in Evelyn's memory, like making her ravioli.

But cooking ravioli wasn't going to help pull me out of this. That was for sure.

By the time my story was set to be published the first week of December, I was an emotional wreck.

Sue asked me over and over again if I wanted to go forward with it and I said yes, but I'm not sure that I ever meant it.

I just didn't want to disappoint anyone or let anyone down.

I planned to take the day off after the story appeared. I didn't want to have to discuss it with my co-workers or anyone else.

When the story appeared that first Sunday in December, the reaction was overwhelming.

Readers shared their stories about caring for parents.

The story struck a chord with so many.

For a short time, I felt as though some good had come from this, that it gave us all reason to believe that we could eventually dig ourselves out of the pain of losing our parents.

I responded to each person who contacted me by phone, email, text or on social media.

I sobbed through each message, reading their stories and thinking about mine.

But as the days wore on, my torment remained with me day and night.

It was inescapable.

When I was out on an interview, someone inevitably would ask if I was "the person who wrote the story about their mother in the nursing home."

And time after time I had to rehash the experience.

I'd do my best to hold it together as I retold the story.

Sometimes I succeeded.

Other times, I didn't.

Life went on.

I did my job.

I took care of my home.

I got up every day, got dressed and functioned … but only barely.

Eight months later, on a Friday afternoon in August, Sue phoned to tell me that she had just received word that our story had been awarded a national Edward R. Murrow Award, one of journalism's top honors.

I didn't even know that Sue had submitted the story for the award.

Team JoAnne was still at work.

Hanging up the phone, I think I was in a state of shock.

I thought of my parents. I thought of all that I had been through. I thought about how proud they would be of me for telling their story.

Tears flowed that day for them, for me, for all that led up to this moment.

That fall, Perry and I met my sisters Ruth and Rose and her boyfriend Mark in New York City for the Murrow awards gala at Gotham Hall, a sprawling, elegant venue just steps from Broadway in midtown Manhattan.

It was a magical, black-tie evening with all the top names in print and broadcast journalism gathered under one roof to honor the best in our business.

As I walked up to the stage to receive the award that night, I felt a rush of memories of Charles Morris and of my parents come back to me.

Even then, on what would be the biggest night of my career, I felt an overwhelming sadness and regret that the two people who followed every moment of my journey to becoming a journalist weren't there to witness the biggest validation of all that I deserved to be a member of this profession that I loved so much.

As I walked back to my seat that night, I wanted to look out and see my mom and dad sitting there.

After all, this was their award, too. They're the ones who taught me the value of a hard day's work and to never quit, even when the odds seem hopelessly stacked against me.

That last lesson came in awfully handy during my toughest days at Charles Morris.

Later, as the gala wound down and Perry and I walked out into the crisp fall air of the city, I clutched that glass award to my chest and once again thought of them.

As I said goodnight to my sisters, I felt my parents' presence on that street in the middle of New York City.

I knew they were there, holding hands and cheering me on, just the way they had my entire life.

Chapter 12 –

Honesty

I'D LIKE TO SAY THAT 2 ½ years after Evelyn's death, as I am writing this book, I have emerged from my grief and life is back to normal.

I'd be lying.

Grief is a constant in my life.

Some days I feel held hostage by it, wanting to break free, but not able to untangle myself from its grip.

A snapshot of the past two-plus years provides how, despite my best attempts,

I remain mired in my past, sometimes incapable of moving on to my tomorrows.

I still have voicemails from Evelyn that I frequently replay, just to hear her voice.

"Hi Jo, this is Mom," she'd always say on those days when she'd call to see how soon I'd be finished working or when I'd be coming to take her to dinner.

I guess she felt she needed to identify herself just in case I didn't recognize her voice.

No chance of that.

No chance at all.

I wear her clothes.

Things like her favorite houndstooth jacket make me feel close to her.

I'll never throw those clothes away, even when they become threadbare and tattered.

To hear her voice and wear those clothes makes me feel that a part of her is still alive, still with me and I can't relinquish those small links to our past.

A drop or two from her almost-empty bottle of Chanel No. 5 makes me tear up. To her, that bottle represented a rare hint of luxury in an otherwise austere life where her most treasured riches were her husband and kids.

I put up her little Christmas tree from the nursing home in our house for the holidays. It's not much of a tree, but it gives me joy and brings back memories of the times when Evelyn and I would sit in her darkened room and enjoy its twinkling lights.

Some nights, the other residents of Charles Morris would come by to admire our miniature display of Christmas pageantry. They loved it as much as we did, and they'd sit there in their wheelchairs talking to Evelyn about this and that or sometimes they'd say nothing at all. Those tiny lights brought so much pleasure to all of them … and to me.

I dread the beginning of May and the approach of Mother's Day. I stay in bed all day on that once-special holiday, not wanting to celebrate any mother other than mine. I can't see that ever changing.

The candle bearing her photo that burned near her casket in the funeral home now sits next to my home computer, an ever-present reminder of her as I write this book.

These days, I don't really feel an overriding need to leave my house for much and when I do, it's usually to do something related to Evelyn or Charles Morris – a visit with Rosie or lunch with someone from the nursing home.

It's a dramatic departure from my old life when I was out and about all the time.

I did things and went places.

There was joy in my life.

Today, although I go about the business of living my life as best I can, my world is fairly limited. There are moments of joy, but they are far fewer than before.

I go to work and do my job.

I come home to Perry, and we probably talk more than we have in the past 16-plus years, mostly because I'm home and not off taking care of my parents during every free minute of my day.

We go out to Big Jim's or to Mineo's or to Coach's for dinner.

We are more present in each other's lives than we have been for a long time.

Though Perry and I are closer, I'm very conflicted about being around other people.

I feel that I'm forever branded as that "woman who was locked up with her mother for so long in a nursing home."

When I'm out on an assignment, people will ask me about it.

It makes me anxious.

I still get emotional.

I try to control it, but I can't.

But at the same time, I want to tell people what I've been through. I want them to know what I've done, what I've sacrificed and why I did it.

Hence the conflict.

Every now and then, something sets me off.

Often, it's a song on the radio that makes me think of my mom and dad and how much I miss them, although there are some songs that give me hope.

Around the time my dad died, Pittsburgh rapper Wiz Khalifa and Charlie Puth released a hit song, "See You Again."

The song's lyrics remind me that although I miss them terribly, I will be reunited one day with Paul and Evelyn.

As a spiritual person with a deep belief in God, I know that is true and I feel like this song speaks to me and my beliefs:

"It's been a long day without you, my friend
And I'll tell you all about it when I see you again (I'll see you again)
We've come a long way (yeah, we came a long way)
From where we began (you know we started)
Oh, I'll tell you all about it when I see you again (I'll tell you)
When I see you again

The process of writing this book has been more painful than I could have ever imagined, but with my now-retired executive editor, Sue, once again helping me, we've pushed through that pain to tell my story.

It's been a long and tear-filled journey. There have been days when I wondered if I would make it.

I am not exaggerating when I say that I've cried every day that we've worked on this book.

At times, the crying became so intense that Sue called a halt to our work, as she did a few days before Thanksgiving 2022 when I'd spent several days compiling information about my last days with Evelyn.

Those were the saddest and most gut-wrenching days of my life and admittedly, reliving them for the purpose of writing this book took a toll on me.

On a video call that day, Sue looked at me, my face a bright shade of red from crying and my voice raspy and said, "we need to stop …. now."

I stared at her for a moment and through my tears wondered what she was talking about.

"We need to stop, and you need to step away from this for a few days. Go celebrate Thanksgiving with your family and we'll get back to it later. For your sake, we need to stop," she said.

She was right. I needed that break.

As we were writing the chapters of this book, I'd sit for hours at the desk in my bedroom, my only light coming from the dim little lamp I took with me from Evelyn's room at Charles Morris.

In more than two decades, I've probably written the life stories of thousands of people, many of those stories tragic and painful.

But this was my story and the thought of baring my soul, revealing my deepest, darkest thoughts and my most vulnerable moments was terrifying.

I struggled to find the right words. I struggled with revealing too much or too little. I didn't want to offend anyone who had helped me along the way.

Inevitably, my frustration would lead to more tears as I sat there in my bedroom all alone, wondering how I'd ever reach the end of this agonizing experience.

In reality, I guess I've cried every day since Evelyn died, sometimes multiple times a day.

It would strike at the oddest times – at work, in traffic or in line at the grocery store – when something or someone reminded me of her.

After Thanksgiving and a one-week break from the book, I'm sorry to say that the crying didn't stop when Sue and I resumed our work.

During that next eight-hour editing session in Sue's office, I sat on her couch, sobbing through most of the day, as we reviewed a first draft of several chapters.

At one point, I looked at Sue typing away on her laptop as tears ran down my face for what might have been the 20th time of the day.

I was mad.

I'm not sure who I was mad at or even why, but at that moment Sue was the only person available, so I took it out on her.

"You don't even care that I'm crying do, you?" I said, somewhat indignant that she hadn't taken the time to stop and comfort me as she had so many times before.

"You made me cry," I told her, looking for some recognition of my tears.

She stopped what she was doing and looked up at me.

You have to understand that Sue has lost both parents and an older brother, her dad dying very suddenly of a heart attack on Christmas Day when she was just out of college.

She understands grief and she is a compassionate person, and she has been supportive of me through this incredible journey.

But she's been in this business for a long time and she understands that journalists, like so many others operating in constantly changing, often volatile worlds, sometimes have to put emotions aside to focus on the jobs in front of them.

At that point, with a hint of humor, Sue reminded me that if she stopped every time I cried, we might never finish this book adding that, "JoAnne, you cried when I asked you what you had for breakfast in the nursing home. You cried about Frosted Flakes."

"And for the record, I did not make you cry," she said, setting the record straight.

We laughed about it, but maybe that's what I needed at that point.

Maybe I needed a little tough love.

In the days and months since returning to work, I honestly think the good days have outnumbered the bad days.

But the bad days have been really, really bad.

One of the worst came six months after Evelyn died when it was announced in the news that Charles Morris was closing its doors for good.

It was a gut punch.

The place that was my home and my mother's home for so long, the place where Evelyn took her last breath, was closing, a victim of financial woes made worse by the pandemic.

It was if someone said they were coming to tear down my house without asking my permission.

I made some calls to my friends there, the staff, the family of residents and Rosie.

What would happen to my Rosie, who'd had such a peaceful, comfortable life since 2018 at Charles Morris.

When it was first announced, Rosie's son, Bobby, was afraid to tell her.

He knew it would crush her.

Some employees would move to other facilities owned by the same nonprofit, some would go elsewhere. Families would scramble to find new homes for loved ones.

I read these words in the story in my newspaper, but couldn't believe it was happening:

"Deborah Winn-Horvitz, president and CEO of the Jewish Association on Aging, which owns and runs the nursing home, described a trifecta of crises converging to prompt the closure: years-long underfunding of Medicaid reimbursements; a state-wide shift toward at-home and community-based care; and the pandemic hiking expenses while causing revenue to plummet."

"There have been a lot of tears today because everyone does feel like a family here. We have just been starting to talk to our families and residents and staff today, and it's been very, very difficult. It's a very painful decision for us to make."

I could only imagine the tears.

I cried all day.

March 7, 2021, was Evelyn's birthday, the first birthday I would celebrate without her. It was six days short of the one-year anniversary of the 2020 lockdown at Charles Morris.

My friend Jane made wedding soup in honor of what would have been Evelyn's 94th birthday.

What I would have given to sit down and talk with her one more time over a hot bowl of soup.

I loved our talks that were generally about nothing in particular, but always contained a healthy share of laughter.

Evelyn loved to laugh. She loved people and spread a kind of contagious joy that made people love her.

I haven't felt that kind of joy since she left me.

Not far behind her birthday was Easter, which came and went with little fanfare.

There was Good Friday and Palm Sunday and Easter Sunday Mass all without Evelyn in her familiar seat in the front row at St. Rosalia's.

I slogged through it all, not able to fill the enormous void that losing her left in my life.

On that first Mother's Day without Evelyn, a friend, Carol Shrefler, texted me to come over to her house. It was late in the day, and I was in bed when she called. I didn't want to move, but I forced myself to get up and get dressed.

She loved my mom, and she knew how crushing this first Mother's Day without her would be for me.

She was right.

We shared our memories of Evelyn and a ton of chocolate. It made it all so much easier, but I knew that it was the one and only time that I would even try to mark Mother's Day.

There was no sense doing it without my Evelyn there as the guest of honor.

I've heard that grief comes in waves, some are soft, and others come out of nowhere and knock you to the ground.

It seems that just when I'm beginning to feel like I'm OK, one of those emotional tsunamis come along and pound the crap out of me.

Sometimes, I find myself scratching and clawing to get up again.

One of those times was in April 2022 – almost two years after Evelyn's death – when my ongoing battle with my sorrow nearly caused me to leave journalism.

I didn't see it coming.

My editor assigned me to cover the funerals of two 17-year-olds shot and killed in the early hours of Easter Sunday during a jam-packed party of young people at an Airbnb on Pittsburgh's North Side.

The deaths of these two young men had grown to a national story about the escalating incidence of gun violence on the nation's streets.

Watching the grief-stricken friends and family of those teen-agers was almost too much for me to bear.

As the casket of Jaiden Brown was carried from the church, the cries from his heartbroken mother and the sobs from his teen-age friends tore at me.

Watching kids so overwhelmed by grief and heartache that they couldn't even approach the casket of Matthew Steffy-Ross was heart-wrenching.

I didn't want to be there, but I couldn't leave. I had a job to do.

But being surrounded by so much horror and pain evoked memories of how I felt when Evelyn died.

It also transported me back to 1979 when I was just 15 and one of my best friends, Darlene Lankiewicz, was killed by a hit-and-run driver on Centre Avenue in the Uptown section of the city as she was headed to volunteer at a local hospital.

Though that grief never left me, I had been able to learn to live with it until this funeral when without warning, I was overcome by a crippling wave of the same incredible sadness I felt four decades earlier.

Images of the two of them – Darlene and Evelyn – flashed through my mind and it was just too much.

Suddenly, I was back there in that room the night Evelyn died, feeling sick to my stomach from the grim reality of her death.

And in my mind, I was returned to that Lawrenceville funeral home with Darlene's heartbroken family, trying to accept the fact that we would never see her again.

Her younger sister Lorri, whom I interviewed for a story on bereaved siblings, told me Darlene's spirit entered me when she was alive.

"And you made a promise, as did I, to carry her spirit with us," Lorri said.

Inside the funeral home for Matthew Steffy-Ross, as I walked toward his great aunt Bonnie to interview her, my heart felt like it was beating out of my chest. I might have been on the verge of a full-blown panic attack.

As journalists, it's our job to report that news, but this was not the news I wanted to report.

Those stories triggered something inside me and I didn't ever want to be in the position where I felt like that again. I didn't know if other stories might affect me that way but I didn't want to take a chance.

The grief that surrounded me at those funerals, coupled with the pain of losing my parents and my friend, made me want to walk away from the job that I fought so hard to get two decades earlier.

I couldn't report about anyone's grief when I had so much of it in my own life.

And that's a tough one for journalists who unfortunately often find themselves chronicling others' worst moments.

Afterward, I talked to my editor, Ben, and told him I didn't think I wanted to be a journalist any longer.

I just couldn't do it.

I was done. I just couldn't handle the emotional ups and downs that came with doing the job day after day.

I'm fairly sure that I wasn't thinking clearly as I told my boss that I wanted to ditch the career that I clearly loved.

Evidently, Ben also thought it was an extreme reaction, because he immediately talked with his supervisor about it.

Later, our managing editor, Rob Amen, called to talk to me.

I explained my feelings to him, and Rob quietly listened, letting me tell my story before speaking.

Finally, he said he didn't want to see me quit and suggested I take some time off if I felt I needed it.

Take whatever time you need, he said.

We don't want to lose you, he added.

I didn't take time off and I didn't quit, but after a period of self-reflection, the experience did make me realize that I needed to be more honest with myself and the people around me.

I needed to admit that I do have some serious, lingering issues from my time at Charles Morris and from Evelyn's death that I had to confront.

Nothing was going to change until I made that admission, I finally told myself.

I needed to know there was no shame in that acknowledgement or my realization that I couldn't go it alone in addressing my issues.

And I needed to talk about it and not push away those who tried to help.

Friends told me that the intensity of my grief and sadness at this stage more than two years later was not normal and that I needed to think about revisiting a therapist.

And although I initially balked at the idea, they were right.

But I know there will be no quick fix for me and quite likely, I never will be the same JoAnne who walked into Charles Morris on March 13, 2020.

And that too, is OK.

To admit that is a huge step forward.

I don't know that any of us will ever be the same after living through this pandemic and the events of the past few years.

Our experiences shape us, and they can change us, but they can't cripple us and I'm afraid that's what I've been standing by and allowing.

Evelyn and Paul would have hated that.

For all that they went through in their lives, they never once permitted adversity to stop them from living their lives. Every time they were knocked down, they got back up.

Evelyn lost a father, a brother and a child and almost died.

But she went on.

If my dad had given up when times were tough, he would have never made it home from the beaches of Normandy and I wouldn't be here today.

I have a long way to go, but I've taken those first steps of being honest with myself and that has been an epic journey.

I guess the thought of losing so much – including the career I'd fought so hard to build – scared me so much that I had to act.

I'm seeing a therapist these days and this woman has been a savior to me. She understands what I have been through, and she listens when I talk about what is fueling my grief.

We have a long way to go, but we have come so far in a very short time.

I am grateful that she has come into my life.

I feel lighter these days and I feel joy every now and then that has been absent for so long.

Sometimes when we need it most, God steps in and delivers the help that we need just when and where we need it.

One of my sisters gave me a pep talk one day that reinforced that notion and how far she believes I've come.

"Take as long as you need," my sister Ruth said. "It may take you forever. Some people would just lock themselves in a room, but you are putting yourself out there. You are like mom and dad. When bad things happen, you put one foot in front of the other. And that is what you are doing now."

"You may never be what you were before. You will have good days and not-so-good days. You may never get to the point where you have all good days," she added.

Sometimes it takes an older sister to show you the way out of the haze.

Luckily, I've got three of them and an older brother, all who are there to lead me through whatever's ahead of me.

Family really is everything in this world.

And mine's not going anywhere.

Through good times and bad, we're in this together.

We learned that from Evelyn and Paul.

The Final Thoughts

WHEN I WAS 4 YEARS old and the other kids were off to school, my mother and I were left alone to spend our days together.

Our next-door neighbor, Sue Bernabo, would laugh when she told stories about me trailing closely behind Evelyn as she hung clothes to dry on the line strung across our backyard.

As I talked a mile a minute, Evelyn would look down and smile, sometimes answering me.

I was glued to her side, never leaving her out of my sight.

And so it was no surprise to anyone that I was there at her side more than 50 years later when the entire world was brought to its knees by covid-19.

With the pandemic bearing down on us, I knew I had to make a decision.

Should I risk everything in my life to be with Evelyn during this pandemic or risk losing Evelyn?

I chose Evelyn.

No matter what, I would always choose Evelyn.

My parents were my first friends.

Maybe that's why I gravitate toward seniors.

I love seniors and they love me.

My friend Therese Lowery McCurren has known me since those days of following Evelyn around my Greenfield backyard.

When interviewed for this book, Therese said I banished thoughts that I might be lonely or isolated by staying in the nursing home with Evelyn. It was my mission to be there when Evelyn needed me.

To this day, I'm still there for my mom's friend Rosie.

It was emotional for me the first time I saw Rosie after my mom's funeral. It was on my birthday – July 17, 2020 – at that same window where Perry and my brother Dave and I visited with Evelyn on her last Mother's Day.

As I drove up the winding road to Charles Morris the tears came, but I did it for Rosie. I met Bobby and Frani and Rosie and she and I each lifted a hand to the glass and tried to touch each other.

My connection to Rosie is part of what keeps me going.

When I interviewed her about my time in the nursing home, she said she knew I would stay there because "that was you."

"There was no deciding. I mean, she was your loving mother and you loved her with everything that you had. She was like your whole life."

Rosie was correct. And I would make the same decision a million times over because of my connection to my parents, which even my elementary school teacher, Sister Ann Rosalia, noticed.

She said she can picture me from those school days and all the days since, seeing me in church with Paul and Evelyn.

"You are reliable and reliable people always consider their commitment to a person as a promise," Sister Ann said.

There is that "promise" again – the feeling of, 'I will do anything for this person.'

"Knowing your relationship with your mom, it made sense," said Dr. Alissa Cohen, my primary care doctor at UPMC Shadyside Family Health Center and also my parents' doctor. "Was it a bold choice? For sure, yes, but JoAnne, who else would I expect to make a bold choice like that? It wasn't surprising to me."

Dr. Cohen recalled seeing me push Evelyn and then Paul into her office, all of us smiling.

I believe that senior citizens need someone to care about them and they return that love a hundred times over.

That's why I still see Rosie. That's why I stop and hug my grade school classmate Gene's mother, Rose Marie, when Perry and I go to St. Rosalia on Saturday for Mass where I also see friends of my mother, Mrs. Barrett and Mrs. Carr and Mrs. Sciulli. It's also where I'm sure to always stop and talk to the ushers and their wives.

I connect with these older people who have so much wisdom.

Two years ago for Christmas, my sister Ruth's mother-in-law, Mrs. Rooney, gifted me her precious hat-pin collection because she knew I would take care of the pins like I do Evelyn's wedding rings.

Resident care aide Christine Ellis from Schenley Gardens first noticed my special relationship with my parents 14 years ago as she watched me get Evelyn ready for bed.

"Everybody knew the bond you had with your mother and your father," Christine said. "You were there like clockwork every single day."

A colleague, Louie Ruediger and I worked on a project interviewing centenarians. It was my second favorite story – Evelyn's story is the first – in my 25 years with the Tribune-Review.

We felt so many emotions being around them – the Greatest Generation. I attended the 100th birthday celebrations of Julia, Elijah, Marion and Bill and loved meeting Frank and Ruthie.

And I hope to celebrate with Rosie when she reaches 100. She turned 99 in February.

During a visit with Rosie in 2022 there was a storm. Rosie looked out the window and told me it was too bad outside for me to drive home.

She offered for me to stay the night and that she would move over and share her single bed with me. She had never invited anyone else to do that.

Dr. Paul J. Friday, chief of clinical psychology at UPMC Shadyside, described my decision to quarantine with my mother as a simple act of love.

"You didn't see the nursing home as a Petri dish and that you could have caught the virus," he said. "You did what you needed to do, what a devoted daughter would do. You made the emotional decision to not be cut off from your mother. You could have left her, but you didn't."

He compared what I did to the opposite of the movie "Titanic." The captain tried to go around the iceberg and it ripped holes in the side of the ship.

"You didn't try to avoid what was going on with your mother," he said. "You hit it straight on. Some people would have used that as an excuse to not go to the nursing home as opposed to what you did, a 24-hour seven-day-a-week stay. What you did was an act of love."

Though my sister Paula's love for our parents runs as deeply as mine, she's not sure she could have done what I did. To one degree or another, all of my siblings felt the same, but they all agreed that my time with Evelyn was a gift.

"(It) might have been difficult, but it's a privilege many people don't get, especially during that covid time," Paula, a former nurse, mother and grandmother said. "People were dying and no one was able to be with them. You saw it. You felt their soul."

"I don't know how you did it. You never lost faith or hope."

My faith in God kept me strong and patient through a very difficult and trying time, said Dan Dulski, a longtime neighbor, who made my parents dinner a few times a month after Evelyn's stroke.

"You were selfless," Dan said. "You were there for your parents 24/7, for all of their needs. Never once thinking of yourself first. There are not many people who could have done what you did."

A lifelong friend, Patti Banze, believes the effect on Evelyn would have been dire if I hadn't quarantined with her.

"I am convinced she wouldn't have made it very long without you," she said. "I saw that you were all in from the start, which is how and why you were all in at the end."

When my mother died, I felt bad that I had to leave Rosie in the nursing home.

When my mother was slipping away from me, Rosie was there in a way that only a mother can be there for a child.

Rosie is strong and resilient like Evelyn. I believed God delivered her to my life for a reason.

When Evelyn slipped away from me, I went to Rosie and hugged her tiny body so hard. I didn't want to let her go. Rosie loves me as she does her children.

When interviewing her for this book, I asked her how she thought I was navigating my grief, and she answered, "I wish I could take some of that heartache from you."

Thank you Rosie … I love you, I said, crying.

"And I love you JoAnne," Rosie said through tears.

I felt close, so close to Rosie, just like that little girl in the backyard of our house in Greenfield hanging clothes out to dry with her mother. And I felt safe.

— JoAnne Klimovich Harrop

Acknowledgements

I's been said that it takes a village to raise a child.

It also takes a village to write a book, especially for this first-time author.

There are so many people who are part of my village.

As a fashionable person, I think of each of them as being as unique as all the hats I wear.

Each hat completes a specific look.

A fedora is more relaxed while a cloche works best for a business meeting and a velvet topper is for special occasions.

I need all of them to complete me.

They've all contributed to developing my style and are essential parts of my story.

I would not be the JoAnne I am without them.

There is no other place to begin than with my parents, Paul and Evelyn.

They were loving and unselfish. They are part of every chapter of my life.

One of my best friends, Jane Carr-Villella, who has been part of my story since grade school, said it best: "You and your siblings hit the jackpot with Paul and Evelyn."

Speaking of my siblings, I am fortunate to have Rose Klimovich, Dave Klimovich, Paula Montanez and Ruth "Rudy" Rooney as my support system, especially while caring for our parents and during those days I was quarantined in the nursing home with Evelyn.

I am thankful for their significant others, Mark Kolakowski, Cindi Klimovich, Josue Montanez and Gregg Rooney, who were welcomed with open arms by Paul and Evelyn, and always understood our love of family. They never complained if one of my siblings needed to come to Pittsburgh.

II couldn't have asked for better nieces and a nephew in Rachel

(Matthew), Sarah (Taylor), Melissa (David), Joshua (Caroline), Charlotte, Violet (Matthew) and Madeline. I am honored to call Olivia, Shay and Emery my great-nieces and Jackson, Ethan and Mason my great-nephews. I'll be welcoming another great niece in November.

Whatever I wanted to do in life, my husband Perry has never questioned it.

My love for journalism began when I delivered the Pittsburgh Press, an afternoon paper, with my very first friend – Therese Lowery McCurren – in our beloved Greenfield neighborhood. Her family embraced me like one of their own.

I was fortunate to be the sports editor of the Scrivener, the newspaper at the former Sacred Heart High School, under the direction of my teacher and friend, Cindy McNulty.

Peg Stewart, Bill Smith, and Patty Van Horn Shultz were my first editors at the Green Tree Times, the Greenfield Grapevine and the Advertiser/ Almanac — papers where I learned the fundamentals of journalism. Patty and I meet for lunch twice a year to celebrate our birthdays.

At the Tribune-Review, I called then-high school editor Rich Emert every week for months until he finally gave me an assignment to write a story about a basketball player from Upper St. Clair High School more than 25 years ago.

I will be forever indebted to publisher Richard Scaife, who created the Pittsburgh Tribune-Review, where I was hired as its first full-time female sports reporter. It was my dream job.

Sports editors Justice B. Hill and Kevin Smith and high school sports editors Jerry DiPaola and Jeff Martinelli always made my stories better.

Top editors Frank Craig, Bob Fryer, and Jim Cuddy welcomed a woman in sports.

Jim gave me the nickname, "Scoop," after my front-page story about a polo player who had competed at an event in Pittsburgh being killed by his girlfriend.

Former Trib president Ralph Martin once spotted me with my parents during a torrential rainstorm at a Pirates baseball game. He noticed me pushing Evelyn in her wheelchair and Paul with his walker. Ralph told me if they wanted tickets to another game, he would get them into the paper's luxury box at PNC Park.

When I was asked to cover the social scene, I worked with Jean Horne, a well-known society page columnist.

I went on to write about fashion and other arts and entertainment events in the features department for Sally Quinn, Sue Jones, Rebecca Killian and Jonna Miller. They helped me become a stronger writer and reporter.

I worked for news editor Ben Schmitt for several years. He encouraged me every day and helped me grow my career through enterprise reporting. Ben was there for me when writing the story for the Trib about quarantining with my mother became emotionally overwhelming.

Ben, Luis Fabregas, Rob Amen, Rick Monti and Sue McFarland edited that story about my mother and treated it with care. Sue has endured hours of me crying while she was trying to edit this book.

Sean Stipp, Melanie Wass, Frank Carnevale and Chris Benson created a visual design for the story that is unmatched.

Every colleague who worked on that story did so while I was off to the side crying.

I could not have made it 25 years without the support of my colleagues at the Trib.

From reporters to editors to photographers and copy editors and designers, they are my family and part of my story. My current editor, Katie Green, has assigned me stories in features, sports and news, further expanding my journalism world.

I also would like to acknowledge Maxwell King, an author, who was the first person to suggest my story has all the elements of a good book.

To my Charles Morris family: Debbie Winn-Horvitz, Tinsy Labrie, Bobby and Frani Wyner, Kandii Coleman, Kris Cyr, Dani Wintermyer, Nadine Kruman, Carol Straney, Marcellina Hoskowicz, Jillian Stone, Sharyn Rubin, Lynette Lederman and Dr. Donna Knupp, just to name a few. I couldn't have asked for a better place for my mother to live in her final days.

High school friends Patti Banze, Marygrace Koziel Reder and Antoinette Sparte have stuck by me through it all.

Everyone I haven't already mentioned who took the time to be interviewed for this book – Christine Ellis, Rose "Rosie" Wyner, Sister Ann Rosalia, Carol Danhires, Monique Hurt-Jones, Dr. Paul Friday, Cindy Vandergrift, Aunt Pat D'Antonio, Dan and Kathy Dulski, Lorri Lankiewicz, Tracey Nicholas and Bill Klimovich – I sincerely appreciate your input.

To my beloved Big Jim's family where owners Gary Burdick and Blane Volovich and their team of Heather, Scott, Brandy, Natalie, Karen, Toni, Bill,

Connie and Brian start making me a Cosmopolitan when they see me walk in the door to comfort me.

And to Dr. Alissa Cohen, my parents' primary care physician and mine, who dubbed me "Daughter of the Decade," I offer my gratitude for your support and your friendship through the most difficult days of my life.

I also offer thanks to my colleague, Carol Pinto-Smith, who helped scan lots of photos for use in this book.

I also am thankful to attorneys Dave Hickton, Eddie Edwards Jr. and Joe Lawrence, who handled the business side of publishing this book.

And last but never least, the one-and-only Jennifer Bertetto, the Trib president and CEO, who believed not only in this book but in me and my unique bond with Evelyn.